Lonely planet

POCKET

LISBON

TOP EXPERIENCES · LOCAL LIFE

D0712052

REGIS ST LOUIS, KEVIN RAUB

Contents

Plan Your Trip

Elevador de Santa Justa (p64)
MATT MUNRO/LONELY PLANET ©

COVID-19

We have re-checked every business in this book before publication to ensure that it is still open after the COVID-19 outbreak. However, the economic and social impacts of COVID-19 will continue to be felt long after the outbreak has been contained, and many businesses, services and events referenced in this guide may experience ongoing restrictions. Some businesses may be temporarily closed, have changed their opening hours and services, or require bookings; some will unfortunately have closed their doors permanently. We suggest you check with venues before visiting for the latest information.

Lisbon's Top Experiences

Witness the masterpiece of Mosteiro dos Jerónimos (p96)

Trundle along on scenic tram 28E (p72)

Explore history at the Castelo de São Jorge (p76)

Tour a palace of art at the
Museu Nacional de Arte Antiga (p132)

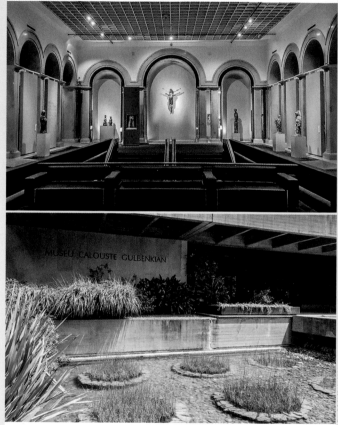

ZABOTNOVA INNA/SHUTTERSTOCK ©

GIANCANA/SHUTTERSTOCK © ARCHITECTS RUY JÉRVIS D'ATHOUGUIA, PEDRO CID AND ALBERTO PESSOA

See the epic art collection of
Museu Calouste Gulbenkian (p120)

Take in stunning tiles at the Museu Nacional do Azulejo (p92)

GREG ELMS/LONELY PLANET ©

FABRREGAS, F AREUVA /GETTY IMAGES ©

Stroll through the Praça do Comércio (p56)

Be awed by the open-sky ruin of the Convento do Carmo (p34)

TICHR/SHUTTERSTOCK ©

JOHNNORTH/GETTY IMAGES ©

Dive into the mammoth Oceanário aquarium (p112)

Catch must-see modern art at Museu Coleção Berardo (p98)

PHOTOSHOOTER2015/SHUTTERSTOCK © ARCHITECTS VITTORIC GREGOTTI AND MANUEL SALGADO

Dining Out

While classics like bacalhau *(dried salt-cod) and* pastéis de nata *(custard tarts) never go out of fashion, the Portuguese capital has raised the culinary bar, with creative, open-minded chefs looking abroad for inspiration. Individualism trumps conformity and restaurants are popping up in the most unlikely places, from convents to pharmaceutical museums and former fish-tackle stores.*

Tasca Charm

Crowded tables, an inviting buzz and menus with robust dishes like *açorda* (bread and shellfish stew) define *tascas*, Lisbon's family-run, cheap-as-chips eateries. Some of the best are tucked away in the backstreets of Baixa, Alfama and Bairro Alto. Find an equally local scene and great value specials at *churrasqueiras* (grill houses).

Fine Dining

Simplicity, pristine ingredients and creativity mark Lisbon's gourmet scene. Chefs such as José Avillez, João Rodrigues and Henrique Sá Pessoa have put the city on the gastro map with ingredient-focused tasting menus, often putting a spin on comfort foods like slow-cooked suckling pig and *bacalhau*.

Cooking Classes

If you're into Portuguese food in a big way and fancy picking up a few tips and tricks from the experts, you can take a class at **Kiss the Cook** (☎ 968 119 652; www. kissthecook.pt; Rua Rodrigues de Faria 103; classes €65). Here you can prepare (and devour) traditional dishes. The classes are totally hands-on and include lunch and wine.

Best Gourmet

Alma Michelin-starred Henrique Sá Pessoa's flagship Portuguese kitchen. (p45)

Loco Chef Alexandre Silva's 'moments' provide a tantalising and unexpected Michelin-starred taste-bud trip through Portugal and beyond. (p139)

Bairro de Avillez Celebrated chef José Avillez' culinary 'neighbourhood' is one-stop satisfaction for foodies. (p43)

Feitoria João Rodrigues elevates seasonal ingredients to a whole new level

SABINO PARENTE/500PX ©

at this riverfront gourmet haunt in Belém. (p108)

Best Tascas & Tabernas

Taberna da Rua das Flores Wildly popular small-plate tavern with daily changing and locally sourced offerings. (p44)

Tasca Zé dos Cornos A family-run favourite in Mouraria serving delectable Portuguese classics. (p85)

Ti-Natércia Moody Alfama gem featuring 'Aunt' Natércia's home-cooked recipes. (p86)

Best for Romance

100 Maneiras Intimate Bairro Alto bistro made for lingering over the

well-executed 10-course menu. (p45)

Flor da Laranja Cosy and romantic Moroccan in Bairro Alto. (p44)

Vicente by Carnalentejana Atmospheric space serving delicacies from the Alentejo. (p43)

Best Bistros

Santa Clara dos Cogumelos A slice of vintage cool in a former market hall, with a mushroom-focused menu. (p86)

Clube das Jornalistas Pared-down elegance in an 18th-century house opening onto a tree-shaded courtyard. (p139)

Best Tapas & Small Plates

Pharmacia Appetising tapas and pharmaceutical fun in Lisbon's apothecary museum. (p44)

Santo António de Alfama Outstanding small plates at this Alfama classic. (p86)

Top Tips 🍽

Couvert, the bread, olives and other goodies automatically brought to the table as appetisers, costs. You pay for what you eat, but it's fine to send it away if you don't want it.

Bar Open

As one local put it, Lisbon is Europe's Havana, with its decadence, bright coloured buildings and party-loving vibe. And whether you're toasting new-found friendships in Bairro Alto's narrow lanes, rocking to live gigs in Cais do Sodré or sipping ginjinha (cherry liqueur) around Rossio at dusk, you can't help but be swept along by the festive spirit in this most sociable of cities.

Nightlife Districts

Take the lead of locals and begin an evening in front of a cubby-hole *ginjinha* bar around Rossio. In the mood for fado? Gravitate towards the medina-like Alfama for the real deal in softly lit, family-run clubs. Bairro Alto is one big street party and bar-hopping after midnight is the way to go. Similarly open-minded, bohemian and oblivious to sleep is sleazy-turned-trendy Cais do Sodré, with a growing crop

of bordello-chic bars and all-night clubs. For a more low-key, gay-friendly vibe in cocktail bars and en-vogue cafes, swing north to Príncipe Real. Edging west of the centre, industrial-cool bars and clubs draw crowds to the riverside in Alcântara.

Best Cocktails

Pavilhão Chinês Lovely elixirs served up in a wacky wonderland setting. (p46)

Foxtrot Unapologetically art-nouveau bar chock-full of atmospheric kitsch and no shortage of creative cocktails. (p140)

Red Frog Bespoke cocktails and classy ambience in a handsomely designed speakeasy. (p128)

Best Wine Bars

BA Wine Bar do Bairro Alto One of Lisbon's best destinations for wine, served up with artisanal cheese and mouth-watering charcuterie. (p45)

O Bar da Odete Great quaffs best enjoyed with delectable Iberian ham. (p66)

Best Rooftops

Park Lisbon's trendiest rooftop bar. (p45)

Memmo Alfama Stupendous views are offered at this boutique hotel bar. (p87)

RADIOKAFKA/SHUTTERSTOCK ©

TOPO Martim Moniz An artsy-leaning lounge with ridiculous castle views. (p66)

Sky Bar Drink in a panorama of Lisbon from this upscale rooftop along Avenida da Liberdade. (p128)

Best Craft Beers

Quimera Brewpub One-of-a-kind beers, including offerings from local brewers. (p140)

Duque Brewpub Featuring 12 taps of Portuguese-only *cerveja artesanal* on an atmospheric Chiado staircase. (p46)

Outro Lardo Easy-going Alfama choice leaning on

Portuguese and Belgian brews. (p89)

Quiosque 8ª Colina Enjoy first-rate brews after a ride on tram 28E, which rattles right past. (p88)

Best Live Music

Mesa de Frades Magical fado in a tiny former chapel. (p89)

A Tasca do Chico A fado favourite in Bairro Alto, with the occasional drop-in taxi driver humming a few bars. (p48)

Damas Graça's eclectic alternative concert hall. (p89)

Zé dos Bois Live music and experimental

performing-arts venue. (p49)

Senhor Fado An intimate and atmospheric fado spot in the heart of the Alfama. (p89)

Best Clubs

Lux-Frágil One of Europe's best megaclubs, a gay-friendly temple of dance alongside the Rio Tejo. (p87)

Bosq Top place for the beauty crowd, and those who simply love to dance. (p140)

Discoteca Jamaica Welcoming hotspot for boogying to some reggae. (p48)

Treasure Hunt

Le freak, c'est retro chic in grid-like Bairro Alto, which attracts vinyl lovers and vintage devotees to its cluster of late-opening boutiques. Elegant Chiado is the go-to place for high-street and couture shopping, to the backbeat of buskers. Alfama, Baixa and Rossio have frozen-in-time stores dealing exclusively in buttons and gloves, tawny port and tinned fish.

Gift Ideas

While there's plenty of tourist tat to be found, Portugal also offers unique wares worth seeking out.

Cork

Portugal is famous for its cork, which is sustainably produced and put to myriad uses (apart from wine bottle stoppers). You'll find cork wallets, handbags, sandals, notebooks, smartphone covers and even umbrellas.

Azulejos

Those exquisite ceramic tiles that adorn so many buildings around Lisbon (both inside and out) make fine souvenirs. The best are hand-painted tiles with one-of-a-kind designs you won't find elsewhere.

Wine

You can pick up some great wines in Portugal, often sold at a fraction of the price you'd pay in your home country. Look for reds from the Alentejo, the Douro and the Dão; semi-sparkling *vinho verde* (great on summer picnics); and one-of-a-kind fortified wines like Moscatel de Setúbal, which comes from the peninsula just south of Lisbon.

Best Gifts & Souvenirs

A Vida Portuguesa Retro sanctuary with the best of Portuguese-designed products, homewares and handicrafts. (p49)

A Arte da Terra A broad selection of authentic Portuguese crafts. (p90)

Best Speciality Stores

Cork & Company Elegant and creative wares fashioned from sustainable cork. (p51)

Claus Porto Exquisitely produced top-end cosmetics, soaps and lotions, all beautifully packaged. (p50)

SALVATOR BARKI/GETTY IMAGES ©

Cortiço & Netos A retro wonderland of industrial *azulejos*, run with passion by three brothers. (p90)

Best Markets

Feira da Ladra Hunt for treasures at this vibrant flea market on Campo de Santa Clara. (p91)

LX Market Popular Sunday market, with everything from food to vintage clothing. (pictured; p141)

Mercado da Ribeira Riverside market hall dating to 1882 with Time Out gourmet food court. (p45)

Best Fashion & Accessories

Kolovrat The flagship store of Lisbon's darling of fashion, Lidija Kolovrat. (p53)

Embaixada Epic 19th-century palace filled with local designers. (p53)

Loja do Burel Colourful and fashionable accessories made with Portuguese mountain wool. (p50)

House of Eleh One of the world's oldest women's shoemakers. (p129)

Best Art & Design

Verso Branco Design store with Portuguese contemporary arts, crafts and furnishings. (p141)

Best Vintage

Outra Face da Lua The perfect spot to browse for a '60s shirt or a vintage prom dress. (p59)

El Dorado Plenty of whimsy and style in this Bairro Alto gem. (p51)

Best Food & Drink

Conserveira de Lisboa A 1930s time warp selling every tinned fish imaginable, all packaged in retro paper. (p59)

Manuel Tavares Doing a brisk trade in cheese, chocolate, port and other Portuguese treats since 1860. (p59)

Manteigaria Silva Slice of a bygone era, this shop specialises in Portuguese staples and delicacies. (p59)

Garrafeira Nacional The be-all and end-all of Portuguese wine. (p68)

Museums & Galleries

The Portuguese capital whispers about its charms, yet it has been hoarding fine art for centuries. You'll find Rodin sculptures and works by Dutch Masters, Dürer and Warhol in its uncrowded galleries, while museums showcasing royal carriages, fado memorabilia and geometric azulejos zoom in on Portugal's rich heritage and history.

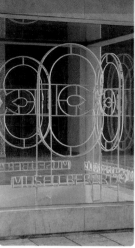

HOLGER LEUE/GETTY IMAGES ©

Best Ancient & Decorative Arts

Museu Calouste Gulbenkian Treasure-trove museum with standout Egyptian artefacts, Rubens paintings and René Lalique jewellery. (p120)

Museu Nacional de Arte Antiga Peerless stash of ancient art, from Dürer originals to bejewelled chalices and Japanese screens. (p132)

Museu de Artes Decorativas Qing porcelain and French silverware in a petite 17th-century palace. (p82)

Casa-Museu Medeiros e Almeida An unsung gem of a private collection in an art-nouveau mansion. (p124)

Best Modern & Contemporary Art

Museu Coleção Berardo Warhol pop art and Picasso cubist wonders crown this outstanding collection. (pictured; p98)

Museu Calouste Gulbenkian – Coleção Moderna Homing in on 20th- and 21st-century art, with works by Hockney, Gormley and Paula Rego. (p124)

Museu Nacional de Arte Contemporânea do Chiado Beautifully converted convent with star pieces by Rodin and Jorge Vieira. (p40)

Best for Heritage

Museu Nacional do Azulejo Piece together 500 years of *azulejo* history. (p92)

Museu Nacional dos Coches A fantasy of fairy-tale coaches in the former royal riding stables. (p103)

Museu de Marinha Circumnavigate the Age of Discoveries studying cannonballs and shipwreck treasures. (p105)

Museu do Oriente Be catapulted back to Portugal's first baby steps in Asia. (p137)

Museu do Fado Tune into the history of fado at this folk-music museum. (p83)

Under the Radar Lisbon

Immerse yourself in a more local scene by heading out of the city centre to untrammelled neighbourhoods far from the tourist crowds. There you'll find some of Lisbon's top ethnic eateries, speakeasy-style drinking dens, little-known overlooks and tiny parks with miraculous secrets, plus a baroque palace that's worth planning a trip around.

IURI S DESIGN/SHUTTERSTOCK ©

Neighbourhood Exploring

Madragoa, west of Baixa, with its narrow lanes and charming restaurants, is reminiscent of Alfama, but with a fraction of the tourists. The once-derelict industrial bairro of Marvila, 4km north of Santa Apolónia, is Lisbon's up-and-coming area and the new domain of cutting-edge art galleries, hip bars and restaurants, and several breweries. The leafy, grid-like Campo de Ourique, 300m west of Estrela, is a somewhat self-contained residential neighbourhood harbouring a wealth of charming sidewalk cafes, independent boutiques and trip-worthy bars and restaurants.

Best Attractions

Miradouro Panorâmico de Monsanto Astounding city-wide panorama set in an abandoned high-society restaurant (pictured).

Palácio dos Marqueses de Fronteira (www.fronteira -alorna.pt) Take a guided tour through an astonishing 17th-century palace.

Campo dos Mártires da Pátria Grassy square with jacaranda trees, a duck pond, cafe and a miracle-working statue.

Best Restaurants & Bars

Mezze (www.facebook.com/ paoapao.associacao) Hummus heaven at this heart-warming Syrian refugee success story.

Izcalli Antojeria (www. izcalli.pt) An authentic journey through Mexico's intricate flavours.

Wine with a View (www. winewithaview.pt) Mobile bar run from a tuk-tuk, serving glasses of Portugal's finest with views of the Tejo.

Viewpoints

Like Rome, Lisbon sits astride seven hills, which equates to a different view for every day of the week. You might huff and puff and curse this hilly town as you climb the umpteenth cobbled calçada (stairway), but take heart: for every stairway there is a beguiling miradouro (viewpoint), for every blister a(nother) breathtaking vista.

SAM74100/GETTY IMAGES ©

Best Bairro Alto Miradouros

Miradouro de São Pedro de Alcântara This tree-shaded terrace has far-reaching views to the castle and the river. (p40)

Miradouro de Santa Catarina Everyone loves these river views, especially at sundown. (p40)

Best Alfama & Graça Miradouros

Largo das Portas do Sol Peer across Alfama's mosaic of red rooftops, spires and domes to the Rio Tejo. (p79)

Miradouro de Santa Luzia Prettily tiled terrace draped with bougainvillea and commanding long views across Alfama and Baixa. (p79)

Miradouro da Senhora do Monte They don't come higher than this pine-shaded viewpoint, affording photogenic perspectives of the castle. (p79)

Miradouro da Graça Popular sunset gathering spot with amazing skyline views. (pictured; p79)

Best Bars with a View

Park A must for sunset gin and tonics. (p45)

Memmo Alfama Look out over cinematic Alfama rooftops. (p87)

TOPO Martim Moniz Alternative, edgy lounge with excellent views of the castle. (p66)

Noobai Café A perfect sunset spot, this terrace has cracking views. (p47)

Sky Bar Lisbon opens out like a pop-up book before you from the Hotel Tivoli Lisboa's sophisticated terrace. (p128)

Top Tips

○ Want to linger? Most of the *miradouros* have kiosk cafes where you can grab a snack.

○ Don't just visit by day: evenings, when the city is aglow, can be just as atmospheric, if not more.

Outdoors

While Lisbon might not immediately strike you as a green city, there are well-tended parks, lush botanical gardens and fountain-dotted praças (squares) offering peaceful respite if you know where to look. For refreshing Atlantic breezes on a summer's day, head to the riverfront where you can stroll, cycle and tick off some of the city's landmarks.

SONIA BONET/SHUTTERSTOCK ©

Beside the Sea

Board a train at Cais do Sodré and within 40 minutes you can be paddling in the Atlantic, licking ice cream and eating just-caught fish in Cascais. Take your pick of its bays or hire a bike from the station to pedal along the coast to the villa-studded resort of Estoril, the 19th-century seaside playground of the rich and famous. Want to catch some waves? Praia do Guincho, 9km northwest of Cascais, attracts surfers, kite-surfers and windsurfers to its wave-lashed beach.

Best Parks & Promenades

Jardim da Estrela Wander among the palms, pines and monkey-puzzle trees. A playground and duck ponds appeal to kids. (p136)

Parque Eduardo VII Gaze across Lisbon to the river from the top of this sloping parterre. (p124)

Ribeira das Naus A gorgeous promenade lopes along Lisbon's revamped riverfront. (p61)

Best Botanic Gardens

Jardim Garcia de Orta A riverside park nurturing colonial flora from dragon trees to frangipani. (p115)

Jardim Botânico Madeiran geraniums, jacarandas and a giant Moreton Bay fig tree thrive in this pocket of greenery north of Bairro Alto. (pictured; p125)

Estufas Take a botanical stroll around this trio of glasshouses, harbouring camellias and coffee and mango trees. (p124)

Best Squares

Praça do Comércio Down by the river, this monumental square is the Lisbon of a million postcards. (p56)

Rossio Wave-like cobbles, fountains, cafes and a 24-hour buzz. (p61)

Jardim do Príncipe Real A giant umbrella of a Mexican cedar shades this plaza, with a kids playground and open-air cafe. (p53)

Pastelarias & Cafes

Sweet tooth? One visit to Lisbon's pastelarias (pastry shops) and you'll be hooked, we swear. Perhaps by the pastéis de nata (caramelised custard tarts that crumble just so); perhaps by the sumptuous gilt and stucco surrounds of old-world cafes; perhaps by the new-generation bakeries doing a brisk trade in French patisserie and cupcakes that are (almost) too pretty to eat.

MATT MUNRO/LONELY PLANET ©

Best Old-School Pastelarias

Antiga Confeitaria de Belém Lisbon's best *pastéis de nata* since 1837. (p105)

Versailles Rather grand 1930s patisserie frequented for cream cakes and gossip. (p126)

Confeitaria Nacional A legendary spot in the heart of the Baixa. (pictured; p59)

Best Sweet Temptations

Bettina & Niccolò Corallo Heavenly chocolates made by a family from São Tomé and Príncipe. (p53)

Fábrica das Verdadeiras Queijadas da Sapa Famous for its *queijadas* (cheesecakes) since 1756. One delicious bite and they're gone. (p143)

Landeau Divine chocolate cake. Enough said. (p48)

Manteigaria Born-again butter factory with *pastéis de nata* to blow you away. (p48)

Best Cafes with a View

Lost In A taste of India and captivating castle views await at this well-hidden, colour-charged cafe. (p42)

Le Chat This glass-fronted cafe has fine views of the Alcântara docks. (p140)

Noobai Café Santa Catarina cafe with a tucked-away terrace for sundowners and twilight city views. (p47)

Best Relaxed Cafes

Pois Café This boho cafe has a laid-back vibe, creative salads and sandwiches. (p84)

Esplanada Café Birdsong, people-watching and a giant cedar tree for a parasol. (p53)

Fábulas A fantasy fairy tale of a cafe, with a mellow vibe and appetising light bites. (p42)

For Kids

Keeping the kids amused in Lisbon is child's play. Even the everyday can be incredibly exciting: custard tarts for breakfast, rickety rides on vintage trams and Willy Wonka–like funiculars. Then there is the castle straight from the pages of a storybook, swashbuckling tales of great navigators in Belém, riverside parks and nearby beaches for free play. As cities go, this is kid heaven.

MIKADUN/SHUTTERSTOCK ©

Kids in Tow

Lisbon has some excellent family deals for those in the know. Many museums and sights offer free entry for under-12s or under 14s, while those under 18 get a 50% discount. Hotels are usually well geared to families and many will squeeze in a cot at no extra charge. We're not going to deny it: the cobblestones make pushchairs hard work, but getting around on public transport is a breeze and under-fours travel free. Kids are welcome in nearly all restaurants and *meia dose* (small portions) are ideal for little appetites.

Best Hands-On Fun

Oceanário Sharks, sea otters and weird and wonderful fish splash around at Europe's second-largest aquarium. (pictured; p112)

Pavilhão do Conhecimento Physics is (finally) a bundle of laughs at this hands-on science centre. (p115)

Castelo de São Jorge A whopper of a castle with ramparts for exploring and a hair-raising history. (p76)

Best Museums

Museu de Marinha Kids can embark on their own voyage of discovery at this barge-stuffed museum. (p105)

Museu Nacional dos Coches Royal coaches that are pure Cinderella stuff. (p103)

Museu da Marioneta Kids love the worldly puppets at this Geppetto's workshop of a museum. (p136)

Best Outdoors

Jardim Botânico Tropical Cool off with your kids in the shade of these botanical gardens in Belém, home to sprawling banyan trees and friendly ducks. (p104)

Jardins d'Água The splashy fun is endless at these water gardens in Parque das Nações. (p115)

Jardim da Estrela Low-key park with duck ponds and an animal-themed playground. (p136)

Tours

SONIA BONET/GETTY IMAGES ©

Culinary Backstreets
(📞963 472 188; www.
culinarybackstreets.com/
culinary-walks/lisbon; 3/6hr
tour €78/105) *Eat Portugal*
co-author Célia Pedroso
leads epic culinary walks
through Lisbon. Try *ginjinha*
(cherry liqueur) then *pastéis
de nata* (custard tarts) and
artisanal sheep cheese,
paired with local wines.

Taste of Lisboa (📞915
601 908; www.tasteoflisboa.
com; experiences €70-85)
Lisbon foodie and radiant
personality Filipa Valente
specialises in neighbour-
hood-centric food tours in
less touristy locales (Campo
de Ourique, Mouraria).

Lisbon Explorer
(📞213 629 263; www.
lisbonexplorer.com; private
group tours €160) Top-
notch English-speaking
guides peel back the many
layers of Lisbon's history
during the three-hour
walking tours offered by this
highly rated outfit.

Lisbon Walker (📞218
861 840; www.lisbonwalker.
com; Rua do Jardim do
Tabaco 126; 3hr walk adult/
child €15/free; ⏰10am)
This excellent company,
with well-informed, English-
speaking guides, offers
themed walking tours of
Lisbon.

Lisbon Cycle Tours
(📞914 173 432; www.
lisboncycletours.com; per
person from €29) Brave the
legendary seven hills of Lisbon on an e-bike, guided by
experienced cyclists through
the old neighbourhoods of
Alfama and Mouraria. You'll
interact with locals, enjoy
fantastic views and indulge
in Portuguese delicacies.

Lisbon Bike Tour
(📞912 272 300; www.
lisbonbiketour.com; adult/
child €32.50/15; ⏰9.30am-
1pm) It's all downhill on this
3½-hour guided bike ride
from Marquês de Pombal
to Belém.

**Underdogs Public Art
Store** (www.under-dogs.
net; Rua da Cintura do Porto
de Lisboa, Armazém A; tours
from €35; ⏰11am-7pm
Tue-Sun) The best option
for Lisbon's street-art tours;
themes include central
Lisbon, greater Lisbon and
Vhils, the artist behind the
Underdogs.

**We Hate Tourism
Tours** (📞913 776 598;
www.wehatetourismtours.
com; Rua Rodrigues de
Faria 103, 4th fl, LX Factory; per person from €30;
⏰2-6pm) Shows a unique
perspective of Lisbon from
inside an open-topped UMM
(a Portuguese 4WD once
made for the army).

HIPPOtrip (📞211 922
030; www.hippotrip.com;
Doca de Santo Amaro;
adult/child €25/15; ⏰9am-
6pm) This fun 90-minute
tour takes visitors on a
land and river excursion
in an amphibious vehicle
that drives straight into the
Rio Tejo!

LGBTIQ+

The kings and queens of Lisbon's gay and lesbian scene are the bear-leaning bars of hip Príncipe Real and the street-party atmosphere of more varied venues around Bairro Alto's so-called 'gay corner' at Rua da Baroca and Travessa da Espera. The big events worth looking out for are Lisbon Pride (www.portugalpride.org) in June and the Festival Internacional de Cinema Queer (www.queerlisboa. pt) in late September.

RFRANCA/GETTY IMAGES ©

Best LGBTIQ+ Nightlife

WoofLX (www.facebook. com/wooflx; Rua da Palmeira 44A; ⏰10pm-4am) Príncipe Real's bear-ish gay bar (though it attracts all shapes and sizes).

Corvo (www.corvo principereal.pt; Calçada Miguel Pais 18; ⏰4pm-2am Tue-Thu, to 3am Fri & Sat) Hipsterish option in Príncipe Real.

Bar TR3S (www.areis marcos.wix.com/tr3slisboa; Rua Rubén a Leitão 2; ⏰4pm-2am Sun-Thu, to 3am Fri & Sat) Bears and friends flock to this hopping bar with outdoor seating.

Shelter Bar (www. facebook.com/shelter barlisboa; Rua da Palmeira 43A; ⏰6pm-2am Sun-Thu, to 3am Fri & Sat) Good for craft beer, Italian-style bites and happy-hour specials.

Clube da Esquina (www. facebook.com/clube daesquina.bairroalto; Rua da Barroca 30; ⏰7pm-2am Mon-Thu, to 3am Fri & Sat, 9pm-2am Sun; 📶) The anchor of Lisbon's 'gay corner' in Bairro Alto.

Posh (www.facebook.com/ poshlisbonclub; Rua de São Bento 157; ⏰midnight-6am Sat) Nightclub with drag, electronic music and big stars.

Construction (📞213 430 040; www.facebook. com/construction.lisbon; Rua Cecílio de Sousa 84; ⏰midnight-6am Fri & Sat) A top club for thirty-somethings, with pumping house music and a dark room.

Finalmente (📞213 479 923; www.finalmenteclub. com; Rua da Palmeira 38; ⏰midnight-6am) Popular club with a tiny dance floor, nightly drag shows and wall-to-wall crowds.

Purex (www.facebook. com/purexclub; Rua das Salgadeiras 28; ⏰10pm-2am Tue-Thu, to 3am Fri & Sat) Unsigned Bairro Alto spot draws a lesbian and mixed crowd.

Trumps (📞915 938 266; www.trumps.pt; Rua da Imprensa Nacional 104B; ⏰midnight-5am Thu, to 6am Fri & Sat) Lisbon's hottest younger-leaning gay club.

Four Perfect Days

Day 1

YATO KENSHIN/SHUTTERSTOCK ©

Start the day with a scenic ride on **tram 28E** (pictured; p72) from Praça do Comercio. Hop off to scale the ramparts of **Castelo de São Jorge** (p76) before strolling the picturesque lanes of Alfama. Afterwards, grab a coffee with a view at **Largo das Portas do Sol** (p79) and get an earful of Lisbon's soulful soundtrack at the **Museu do Fado** (p83).

In the afternoon, continue on to the fortress-like **Sé de Lisboa** (p83) en route to shopping in pedestrianised Baixa. Head up to the top of **Arco da Rua Augusta** (p57) for a unique perspective of Lisbon.

Round out the evening back in lantern-lit Alfama over fado at the charming **Mesa de Frades** (p89).

Day 2

MATT MUNRO/LONELY PLANET ©

Head to Belém for pastries at **Antiga Confeitaria de Belém** (p105) before visiting local spots like the fantastical **Mosteiro dos Jerónimos** (p96), the intricately carved **Torre de Belém** (p103) and the avant-garde **Museu Coleção Berardo** (p98). Enjoy a late lunch at **Enoteca de Belém** (p107).

Spend the afternoon exploring Belém's other excellent museums such as the **Museu de Arte, Arquitetura e Tecnologia** (p103). Afterwards, enjoy a sundowner at the riverside **A Margem** (p108).

Head back to the city centre for a fabulous meal at **100 Maneiras** (p45), then take in a bit of nightlife in Bairro Alto. End the night down in Cais do Sodré, with first-rate cocktails and great atmosphere at **Pensão Amor** (p37).

CAVAN IMAGES/SHUTTERSTOCK © / ARCHITECT PETER CHERMAYEFF

ALEX BUTLER/LONELY PLANET ©

Day 3

Spend the morning window-shopping and cafe-hopping in well-heeled Chiado. Browse unique gift ideas at **A Vida Portuguesa** (p49) and **Apaixonarte** (p51), then visit the evocative earthquake-scarred ruins of the **Convento do Carmo** (p34). Have lunch at the outstanding **Bairro de Avillez** (p43).

Book a walking or street-art tour for the afternoon, or head for futuristic Parque das Nações, where you can take a ride on the **Teleférico** (p115) or visit the excellent **Oceanário** (pictured; p112).

In the evening, ask for a table for a view at **Chapitô à Mesa** (p85). Then head out for a big night of dancing amid eclectic sounds in clubbing temple **Lux-Frágil** (p87).

Day 4

On day four, start the morning with a visit to the **Museu Nacional de Arte Antiga** (p132), home to one of Lisbon's best art collections. Afterwards, head over to the **Museu do Oriente** (p137) for a look at treasures from Asia. Have lunch and go window-shopping in the hip **LX Factory** (pictured; p141).

In the afternoon, explore Baixa: take a stroll through **Praça do Comércio** (p56), head underground at **Núcleo Arqueológico da Rua dos Correeiros** (p61) and get a history lesson at **Lisbon Story Centre** (p61). Later, have a seafood feast at **Solar dos Presuntos** (p66).

If you have any energy left, head to nightlife-loving Bairro Alto for cocktails in eclectic drinking dens like **O Bom O Mau e O Vilão** (p47) or the rooftop perch of **Park** (p45).

Need to Know

For detailed information, see Survival Guide p145

Currency
Euro (€)

Language
Portuguese

Visas
EU nationals need no visa. US, Canadian, Australian, UK and NZ visitors can stay for up to 90 days with no visa.

Money
ATMs widely available. Credit cards generally accepted, but cash preferred in some small shops and restaurants.

Mobile Phones
European and Australian mobile phones work. US visitors should check with their service provider. Cut the cost of roaming charges by buying a local SIM card.

Time
Lisbon is on GMT/UTC.

Tipping
Tip 5% to 10% if you are satisfied with the service. *Serviço* (service charge) is usually only included in the bill at top-end restaurants.

Daily Budget

Budget: Less than €65
Dorm bed: €18–35

Fixed-price meal: €7–10

Lisboa Card for unlimited transport and admission discounts: €19

Midrange: €65–160
Double room in a central hotel: €60–120

Meal in a midrange restaurant: €20–30

Walking or cycling tour of the city: €15–35

Top end: More than €160
Boutique hotel room: from €120

Three-course dinner with wine: from €50

Night at a fado club: €50

Useful Websites

Lonely Planet (www.lonelyplanet.com/lisbon) Destination information, hotel bookings, traveller forum and more.

Visit Lisboa (www.visitlisboa.com) Comprehensive tourist office website.

Lisbon Lux (www.lisbonlux.com) Trendy city guide.

Spotted by Locals (www.spottedbylocals.com/lisbon) Insider tips.

Advance Planning

One month before Book excursions, top-end restaurants, theatre and opera tickets.

Two weeks before Buy tickets for gigs and reserve a table in a fado club.

A few days before Check out what's happening on event websites and bone up on your Portuguese wine knowledge on www.viniportugal.pt.

Arriving in Lisbon

Most international visitors arrive at Lisbon Airport (www.ana.pt), 8km northeast of the city.

✈ From Lisbon Airport

Convenient metro access to downtown from Aeroporto station; change at Alameda (green line) for Rossio and Baixa. A taxi for the 15-minute ride into central Lisbon costs around €16 (plus €1.60 for luggage). Alternatively, buy a pre-paid voucher to any address from Ask Me Lisboa in Arrivals. Uber and other app-based taxis pick up outside Departures (not Arrivals) and are considerably cheaper. You can also catch the Aerobus, which departs from outside Arrivals (adult/child €3.60/2, 25 to 35 minutes, roughly every 20 minutes from 7am to 11pm).

Getting Around

Lisbon's public-transport system is a bit of a mess, but is cheap and does the job. For timetables, routes and fares, see www.carris.pt and www.metrolisboa.pt.

Ⓜ Metro

Lisbon's subway is the quickest way around. Runs from 6.30am to 1am. Single tickets cost €1.45.

🚋 Tram

The best way to get up into hilltop neighbourhoods (Alfama, Castelo, Graça) and western neighbourhoods (Estrela, Campo de Ourique). Runs from 5am/6am to about 10pm/11pm.

🚌 Bus

Particularly good for reaching Príncipe Real, but the extensive network runs throughout the city. Buses operate from 5am/6am to about 10pm/11pm.

Lisbon Neighbourhoods

Marquês de Pombal, Rato & Saldanha (p119)

Top-drawer museums, pristine gardens and some of Lisbon's best restaurants lure you north to these lesser-known neighbourhoods.

Estrela, Lapa & Alcântara (p131)

A world-class ancient art museum, streets with low-key, leafy charm and dockside nightlife entice in these neighbourhoods.

Belém (p95)

Manueline monuments, a Unesco-listed monastery and contemporary art await in this nautical-flavoured neighbourhood by the river.

Museu Nacional de Arte Antiga
◉

Mosteiro dos
◉ *Jerónimos*
◉ *Museu Coleção Berardo*

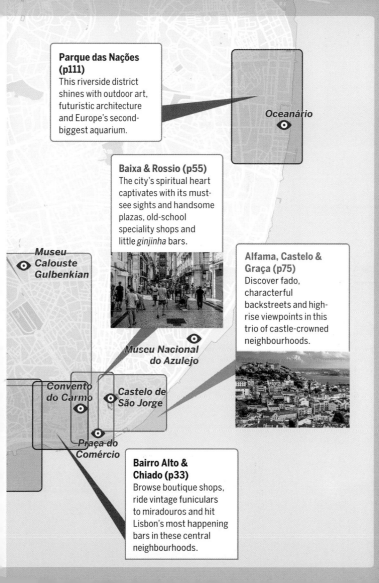

Parque das Nações (p111)
This riverside district shines with outdoor art, futuristic architecture and Europe's second-biggest aquarium.

Oceanário 👁

Baixa & Rossio (p55)
The city's spiritual heart captivates with its must-see sights and handsome plazas, old-school speciality shops and little *ginjinha* bars.

Alfama, Castelo & Graça (p75)
Discover fado, characterful backstreets and high-rise viewpoints in this trio of castle-crowned neighbourhoods.

Museu Calouste Gulbenkian 👁

👁 *Museu Nacional do Azulejo*

Convento do Carmo 👁

👁 *Castelo de São Jorge*

Praça do Comércio

Bairro Alto & Chiado (p33)
Browse boutique shops, ride vintage funiculars to miradouros and hit Lisbon's most happening bars in these central neighbourhoods.

Explore
Lisbon

Explore ✦

Bairro Alto & Chiado

Two neighbourhoods, two very different personalities. Chiado invites days spent boutique-shopping, gallery-hopping and lingering in literary cafes. Its more rakish, party-loving neighbour is Bairro Alto, a tangle of lanes harbouring dozens of shabby-chic shops, late-night bistros and hole-in-the-wall bars. Swinging south, Cais do Sodré has reinvented itself from red-light district to nightlife hub.

○ **Mercado da Ribeira (p45)** Overwhelming yourself in one of Europe's best gourmet food courts.

○ **Igreja & Museu São Roque (p40)** Admiring the dazzling interior of gold, marble and Florentine azulejos at this 16th-century Jesuit church.

○ **Convento do Carmo (p34)** Getting wowed upon entering the roofless remnants of this survivor of the 1755 earthquake.

○ **BA Wine Bar do Bairro Alto (p45)** Chasing exceptional artisanal cheeses and charcuterie with equally impressive wines at our favourite Lisbon wine bar.

Getting There & Around

Ⓜ The green and blue lines stop at Baixa-Chiado; the green line runs to Cais do Sodré.

🚊 Trams 15E and 18E stop at Cais do Sodré and tram 25E at Rua de São Paulo. 28E is convenient for Santa Catarina.

🚌 Bus 758 (Cais do Sodré–Benfica) stops at the Ascensor da Glória and Príncipe Real.

Neighbourhood Map on p38

Ascensor da Glória (p41) KATATONIA82/GETTY IMAGES ©

Top Experience 📷

Be Awed by the Open-Sky Ruin of the Convento do Carmo

⊙ MAP P38, F4

Soaring ethereally above Lisbon, the convent, founded in 1389, was all but devoured by the 1755 earthquake. Its shattered pillars and wishbone-like arches are completely exposed to the elements. The 19th-century taste for romantic ruins meant it was never restored, and it later became the archaeology museum you see today.

www.museuarqueologico docarmo.pt

Largo do Carmo

adult/child €4/free

🕙10am-7pm Mon-Sat Jun-Sep, to 6pm Oct-May

Nave

Open to the sky, the nave is scattered with evocative tombstones, statues, baptismal fonts and coats of arms. Look for the Renaissance loggia from Santarém, the Manueline window from the Mosteiro dos Jerónimos, 6th-century Hebraic funerary stelae and the baroque statue of St John Nepomucene from the old Alcântara bridge.

Main Chapel

First up in the captivating archaeology museum is the main chapel, decorated with three baroque *azulejo* (hand-painted tiles) panels. It shelters the tomb of Nuno Álvares Pereira, who had the convent built to trumpet Portuguese victory in the 1385 Battle of Aljubarrota, alongside the early-14th-century tomb of Fernão Sanches, vividly depicting a boar hunt.

Pre-Columbian Treasures

Aztec statues, Chimu ceramics, Inca zoomorphic pottery and a trio of mummies – one battered Egyptian and two gruesome 16th-century Peruvians – are on display in room 4. The blue-and-white *azulejos* depict scenes from the Passion of Christ.

Roman-Moorish Collection

Roman milestones, funerary stelae and sarcophagi are showcased alongside later finds like a 6th-century Visigothic belt buckle in room 2. Two pillars adorned with griffins and a lion frieze are among the medieval Moorish standouts.

Prehistoric Finds

In room 1 you can zip back to prehistoric times contemplating Palaeolithic hand axes, neolithic pottery, megalithic tomb objects and chalcolithic artefacts like loom weights.

★ Top Tips

o Pick up a free map at the entrance to pinpoint the key exhibits.

o For the best photographs of the convent perched on the hillside, head down to Rossio.

o Don't miss the stunning view of Lisbon and Castelo de São Jorge from the museum shop.

o Free 30-minute guided tours in Portuguese run daily at noon and 5pm.

✖ Take a Break

Revive over pastries, *tartines* (open sandwiches) and lunch specials at **Tartine** (www.tartine.pt; Rua Serpa Pinto 15; mains €4.50-14; ☘ 8am-8pm Mon-Fri, 10am-8pm Sat; ☏), a couple of minutes' stroll away.

On the backside of the convent, **TOPO Chiado** (Terraços do Carmo; ☘ 12.30pm-midnight Sun-Wed, to 2am Thu-Sat) shakes and stirs cocktails on an outdoor lawn with stunning views.

Walking Tour 🥾

Cais do Sodré Bar Crawl

For years, riverside Cais do Sodré's backstreets were the haunt of whisky-slugging sailors craving after-dark sleaze. But in 2011 the district was upgraded from seedy to stylish. Rua Nova do Carvalho was painted pink and the call girls were sent packing, but the edginess and decadence on which Lisbon thrives remain in this bairro (neighbourhood) that's perfect for a late-night bar crawl.

Walk Facts

Start Cafe Tati;
Ⓜ Cais do Sodré

End Musicbox;
Ⓜ Cais do Sodré

Length 500m; 2–3 hours

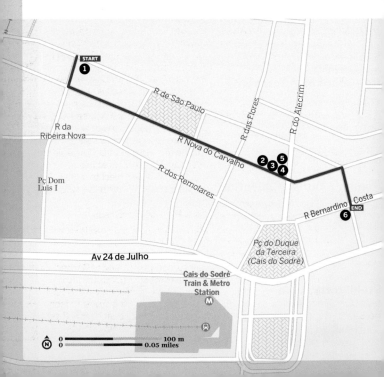

❶ Gin & Tonic Time

Begin an evening in mellow fashion at the small and intimate **A Tabacaria** (Rua de São Paulo 75; 6pm-2am Sun-Wed, 6am-3am Thu-Sat). Order a refreshing gin and tonic (made with unique house-macerated tinctures) and enjoy it with the crowd that spills onto the pavement.

❷ Tinned-Fish Tapas

As you stroll down Rua Nova do Carvalho, stop in at tiny **Sol e Pesca** (www.solepesca.com; Rua Nova do Carvalho 44; tinned fish €2-16.80; ☺noon-2am Sun-Thu, to 3am Fri & Sat). Rods, hooks and nets give away its former life as a fishing-tackle shop. Cabinets are stacked with vintage-looking cans of sardines, tuna and other tinned seafood, or '*conservas*' as the Portuguese say. Grab a chair, order a tin or two, and accompany it with bread, olives, wine and good company.

❸ Rising Fado Stars

When it comes to fado (see box p88), it can be hard to find the real deal. Well, **Povo** (☎213 473 403; www.povolisboa.com; Rua Nova do Carvalho 32; small plates €6.40-14.30; ☺6pm-2am Sun-Wed, to 4am Thu-Sat) is it. A different *fadista* (fado singer) is in residence every month, there is no stage, *petiscos* (tapas) are served, and the aim is to give young, little-known singers exposure. The fado stars of tomorrow? Hear them here first.

❹ Gigs Under the Bridge

Tucked under the arches of the bridge, the cave-like **Musicbox** (www.musicboxlisboa.com; Rua Nova do Carvalho 24; ☺11pm-6am Mon-Sat) is all about the music. This is hands down one of the city's best venues for gigs, and you rarely pay more than €15 for a ticket. Concerts cover the entire spectrum, from jazz to indie, rock, metal and DJs.

❺ Bordello Chic

Take one of the small alleys alongside the bridge to find yourself up on Rua do Alecrím, then look for number 19. If the name **Pensão Amor** (www.pensaoamor.pt; ☺2pm-3am Sun-Wed, to 4am Thu-Sat) doesn't give the game away, the graffiti murals of cavorting nudes and the scarlet walls surely will. A brothel reborn as an art space, it has a bordello-chic bar serving creative cocktails, a bookshop with erotic literature, and boutiques selling lingerie and vintage garb. Concerts, DJs, plays and poetry recitals attract the crowds. Expect to queue at the weekend – it's worth the wait.

❻ A Pint of Portugal

It's not all corsets and crowds in Cais do Sodré. If you're looking for a more relaxed atmosphere, take the short walk to Irish-owned **Crafty Corner** (www.facebook.com/craftycornerlisboa; Tv Corpo Santo 15; ☺4pm-2am Mon-Sat, to 11.45pm Sun; 🛜). It features 12 taps of Portuguese-only craft beer and its leather sofas and somewhat artsy atmosphere are perfect for a pint.

Bairro Alto & Chiado

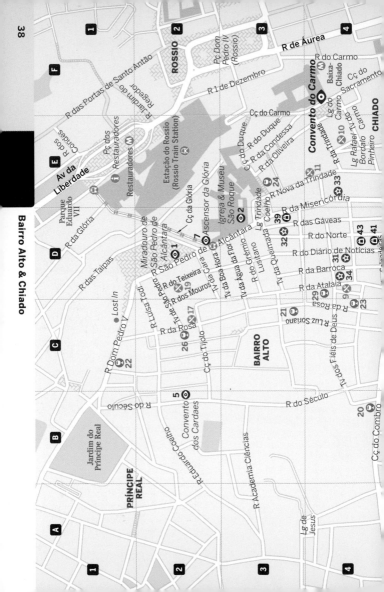

PRÍNCIPE REAL

Jardim do Príncipe Real

BAIRRO ALTO

Convento dos Cardaes 5

Lost In 22

26 17

R da Rosa

R dos Mouros

Tv de São Pedro de Alcântara

Miradouro de São Pedro de Alcântara

R de São Pedro de Alcântara

19

1

Ascensor da Glória

Cç da Glória

7

2 Igreja & Museu São Roque

Estação do Rossio (Rossio Train Station)

R 1 de Dezembro

R das Portas de Santo Antão

Pç dos Restauradores

Av da Liberdade

Parque Eduardo VII

R da Glória

R das Taipas

R Luísa Tódi

R Dom Pedro V

R Eduardo Coelho

R do Século

R Academia Ciências

Lg de Jesus

Cç do Combro

20

R da Luz Soriano

Tv dos Fiéis de Deus

R da Atalaia

29

R da Barroca

34

R do Diário de Notícias

31

R do Norte

43

41

R das Gáveas

R da Misericórdia

33

R Nova da Trindade

24

R da Oliveira

R da Condessa

R do Duque

Cç do Duque

Cç do Carmo

R do Carmo

Convento do Carmo

Lg do Carmo

10

R da Trindade

Lg Rafael Bordalo Pinheiro

CHIADO

Baixa-Chiado

Cç do Sacramento

R de Áurea

ROSSIO

Pç Dom Pedro IV (Rossio)

Restauradores

Tv da Boa Hora

R do Grémio Lusitano

Tv da Queimada

Lg Trindade Coelho

32

39

21

23

R da Rosa

Cç do Tijolo

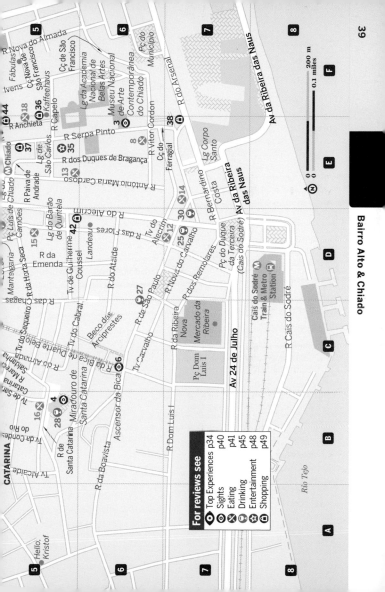

Bairro Alto & Chiado

Fábulas
R Nova do Almada
Cç Nova de São Francisco
tvens
44
18
36
Kaffeehaus
R Anchieta
R Capelo
Lg da Academia Nacional de Belas Artes
Museu Nacional de Arte Contemporânea do Chiado
3
Pç do Município
Cç de São Francisco
R do Arsenal

37
35
R Serpa Pinto
R dos Duques de Bragança
R Vítor Cordon
Lg de São Carlos
8
Ferragial
38
Lg do Corpo Santo

13
R Paiva de Andrade
R António Maria Cardoso
Cç do
R Bernardino Costa
Av da Ribeira das Naus

Pç Luís de Camões
Lg do Barão de Quintela
42
Landeau
R do Alecrim
14
R da Ribeira das Naus

15
R da Emenda
R das Flores
12
25 30
R Nova do Carvalho
Pç do Duque da Terceira (Cais do Sodré)

Mantgaria
Tv de Guilherme Coussel
Tv do Alecrim
R Nova do Carvalho

R da Horta Seca
R do Ataíde
27
R de São Paulo
R dos Remolares
Cais do Sodré Train & Metro Station

R das Chagas
Beco das Arciprestes
Tv do Cabral
Tv Carvalho
R da Ribeira Nova
R Cais do Sodré

R do Sequeiro
Tv da Bica de Duarte Belo
6
Mercado da Ribeira

R Marechal Saldanha
Ascensor da Bica
Pç Dom Luís I

Tv de San Catarina
R do Almada
Miradouro de Santa Catarina
Av 24 de Julho

16
28 4
R de Santa Catarina
R da Boavista
R Dom Luís I

CATARINA
Tv do Rio
R de

Tv Alcaíde
Hello, Kristof

Rio Tejo

For reviews see
◉ Top Experiences	p34	
◉ Sights	p40	
✖ Eating	p41	
☕ Drinking	p45	
◉ Entertainment	p48	
🛍 Shopping	p49	

N
0
0
200 m
0.1 miles

A B C D E F

5 6 7 8

Sights

Miradouro de São Pedro de Alcântara VIEWPOINT

1 🎯 MAP P38, D2

Hitch a ride on vintage **Ascensor da Glória** (p41) from Praça dos Restauradores, or huff your way up steep Calçada da Glória to this terrific hilltop viewpoint. Fountains and Greek busts add a regal air to the surroundings, and the open-air kiosk doles out wine, beer and snacks, which you can enjoy while taking in the castle views and live music. (Rua São Pedro de Alcântara; ⊙viewpoint 24hr, kiosk 10am-midnight Sun-Wed, to 2am Thu-Sat)

Igreja & Museu São Roque CHURCH, MUSEUM

2 🎯 MAP P38, D3

The plain facade of 16th-century Jesuit Igreja de São Roque belies its dazzling interior of gold, marble and Florentine *azulejos* – bankrolled by Brazilian riches. Its star attraction is **Capela de São João Baptista**, a lavish confection of amethyst, alabaster, lapis lazuli and Carrara marble. The **museum** adjoining the church is packed with elaborate sacred art and holy relics. (www. museu-saoroque.com; Largo Trindade Coelho; church free, museum adult/child €2.50/free, free 10am-2pm Sun; ⊙2-7pm Mon, 10am-7pm Tue, Wed & Fri-Sun, 10am-8pm Thu, shorter hours in winter)

Museu Nacional de Arte Contemporânea do Chiado MUSEUM

3 🎯 MAP P38, E6

Art fans flock to Museu do Chiado, housed in the strikingly converted Convento de São Francisco. While the gallery's permanent collection of 19th- and 20th-century works features pieces by Rodin, Jorge Vieira and José de Almada Negreiros, you won't see them unless they have made their way into the temporary-only exhibitions. (MNAC; www.museuartecontemporanea.pt; Rua Serpa Pinto 4; adult/child €4.50/free; ⊙10am-6pm Tue-Sun)

Miradouro de Santa Catarina VIEWPOINT

4 🎯 MAP P38, B5

Students bashing out rhythms, pot-smoking hippies, stroller-pushing parents and loved-up couples all meet at this precipitous viewpoint in boho Santa Catarina. The views are fantastic, stretching from the river to the Ponte 25 de Abril and Cristo Rei. (Rua de Santa Catarina; ⊙24hr)

Convento dos Cardaes CONVENT

5 🎯 MAP P38, B2

The inconspicuous, graffitied white facade of this 17th-century fort-like convent contrasts with the rich blue-and-white tiles and gilded carvings of the church inside. As one of the few buildings that remained intact after the 1755 earthquake, the convent is a rare example of the Portuguese baroque style in Lisbon. Guided tours take about an hour. (www. conventodoscardaes.com; Rua do Século 123; adult/student/child €5/4/ free; 2.30-5.30pm Mon-Sat)

Ascensor da Bica   FUNICULAR

6 ⊙ MAP P38, C6

This funicular has been creaking arthritically up the steep, narrow Rua da Bica de Duarte Belo since 1892. Jump aboard to save your legs and enjoy fleeting glimpses of the Rio Tejo and pastel-hued houses. (www.carris.pt/pt/ ascensores-e-elevador; Rua de São Paulo; return trip €3.70; 7am-9pm Mon-Sat, 9am-9pm Sun)

Ascensor da Glória   FUNICULAR

7 ⊙ MAP P38, D2

Lisbon's second-oldest funicular has been shuttling folk from Praça dos Restauradores to Rua São Pedro de Alcântara since 1885. Knockout views await at the top. (www.carris.pt/pt/ascensores-e-elevador; Calçada da Glória; return €3.70; 7.15am-11.55pm Mon-Thu, to 12.25am Fri, 8.45am-12.25am Sat, 9.15am-11.55pm Sun)

Eating

Ao 20 – Vegan Food Project   VEGAN €

8 ⊗ MAP P38, E6

So good it even lures in devout carnivores, this small, hip and bustling vegan place offers two elabo-

Igreja de São Roque

Bairro Alto & Chiado Cafe Culture

This area has a crop of boho-flavoured cafes good for whiling away an afternoon or evening. At the wonderfully relaxed **Fábulas** (Map p38, F5; www.fabulas.pt; Calçada Nova de São Francisco 14; mains €11-17; 12.30pm-midnight Mon & Tue-Thu, to 12.30am Fri & Sat;), exposed stone, cosy nooks and flickering candles conjure a *fábula* (storybook fable). Elegant **Kaffeehaus** (Map p38, F5; www.kaffeehaus -lisboa.com; Rua Anchieta 3; mains €5-15, Sun brunch €9-14; noon-midnight Tue-Sat, to 8pm Sun) is a picturesque spot for coffees and Austrian fare. For drinks and light bites with knockout views, head to the Indo-chic terrace at **Lost In** (Map p38, C1; www.facebook.com/lostin.esplanada; Rua Dom Pedro V 56; 4pm-midnight Mon, from 12.30pm Tue-Sat), shaded by colourful parasols.

Those more interested in high-quality espressos and pour-overs should check out Lisbon's third-wave cafes, including the Scandinavian-inspired **Hello, Kristof** (Map p38, A5; www.hellokristof. com; Rua do Poço dos Negros 103; 9am-6pm Mon-Fri) and Aussie-Portuguese owned **The Mill** (Map p38, A4; www.themill.pt; Rua do Poço dos Negros 1; 8am-6pm Mon-Fri, 9am-5pm Sat & Sun;).

rate, daily-changing chalkboard specials (Manchurian meatballs with tomato, coconut and masala, for example). There's a fixed menu of loaded lentil burgers, beet burgers and veg sandwiches on *bolo do caco* (round bread cooked on a basalt stone slab), plus Lisbon craft beer. (967 989 184; www. facebook.com/ao26veganfoodproject; Rua Vítor Cordon 26; mains €5.50-7.50; 12.30-6.30pm & 7.30-11pm Tue-Sat;)

Tantura

ISRAELI €

9 MAP P38, D4

This Middle Eastern godsend started with a love story: Israeli couple Elad Bodenstein and Itamar Eliyahuo fell in love with

Portugal on their honeymoon and perceptively realised Lisbon needed hummus. A long list of hummus and shakshuka – often embellished with creative touches sourced from Romania, Poland, Iraq and Tunisia – now fills that void exceptionally. Lovely staff as well. (218 096 035; www. tantura.pt; Rua de Trombeta 1D; mains €3.50-11.90; 6.30pm-midnight Tue-Sun;)

Boa-Bao

ASIAN €€

10 MAP P38, E4

The food at this trendy place will transport you to Laos, Cambodia, Malaysia and Vietnam, but the ceramic swallows draped across the exposed brick archway (the most famous artwork of Rafael Bordalo, the artist for which the beautiful Chiado plaza is named) are undeniably Portuguese. (☏919 023 030; www.boabao.pt; Largo Rafael Bordalo Pinheiro 30; small plates €6.50-9, mains €12-18; ⊙noon-11.30pm Sun-Wed, to 12.30am Thu-Sat; 🛜)

Bairro de Avillez   PORTUGUESE €€

11 🍴 MAP P38, E4

Step into this culinary creation from Portugal's most famous chef – Michelin-starred maestro José Avillez – who has set up his gastronomic dream destination as a 'neighbourhood' featuring several dining environments, including everything from a traditional tavern to an avant-garde gourmet cabaret. (☏215 830 290; www.jose avillez.pt/en/bairro-do-avillez; Rua Nova da Trindade 18; small plates €2-16.50, mains €7-18.50; ⊙noon-midnight; 🛜)

Vicente by Carnalentejana   PORTUGUESE €€

12 🍴 MAP P38, D7

This sexy restaurant dishes up succulent beef and pork dishes made with ultra-premium Carnalentejana DOP-certified meat from the Alentejo, along with wines, cheeses, olive oils and other treats produced by the same artisanal farmers. In this former coal shop turned carnivore's den of decadence, the original low-slung stone walls, exposed air ducts and filament light bulbs are notably atmospheric. (☏218 237 126; www.

carnalentejana.pt/restaurantes; Rua das Flores 6; mains €10.50-16.90; ⊙12.30-3pm & 7.30-11.30pm; 🛜)

Mini Bar   FUSION €€

13 🍴 MAP P38, E5

Trendy and fun, Mini Bar is the most approachable and hippest entry point into the innovative cuisine of Michelin-starred chef José Avillez, who has several restaurants in the vicinity. Billed as a gourmet bar amid theatre-inspired decor, it's a trendy mash-up of nightlife and fine dining, where you'll enjoy exceptional craft drinking alongside small, chef-driven petiscos. (☏211 305 393; www.minibar.pt; Rua António Maria Cardoso 58; small plates €2.80-14.50, tasting menus €45-55; ⊙7pm-2am; 🛜)

Casa de Pasto   PORTUGUESE €€

14 🍴 MAP P38, E7

Up the stairs behind a not-very-triumphant facade lies this surprising treasure trove of 19th-century Portuguese bric-a-brac (seashell nightlights, ceramic taxidermy, gaudy mirrors), while Diogo Noronha, a former intern at renowned New York restaurant Per Se and one of Lisbon's top upstart chefs, does decidedly delightful things with his charcoal oven. The duck leg? The grilled mussels? The octopus? Perfect. (☏963 739 979; www.casadepasto.com; Rua do São Paulo 20, 1st fl; mains €14-30; ⊙12.30-3pm & 8-11pm Mon-Wed, to midnight Thu-Sat; 🛜)

Taberna da
Rua das Flores

PORTUGUESE €€

15 MAP P38, D5

You'll have to get past the owner's unfortunate 'My way or the highway' attitude, but if you do, this tiny throwback tavern does a daily-changing, locally sourced chalkboard menu of creative small plates, all market-fresh and fantastic. (213 479 418; Rua das Flores 103; small plates €2.50-15; noon-midnight Mon-Fri, from 6pm Sat)

Pharmacia

MEDITERRANEAN €€

16 MAP P38, B5

At this wonderfully quirky restaurant in Lisbon's apothecary museum, chef Susana Felicidade (Algarvian grandmother-trained!) dispenses tasting menus and tapas singing with flavours that are both market-fresh and Mediterranean influenced. Appetisers served in test tubes, cabinets brimming with pill bottles and flacons – it's all part of the pharmaceutical fun. The terrace is a great spot for cocktails. (213 462 146; www.chef-felicidade.pt; Rua Marechal Saldanha 2; tapas €10-15; 12.30pm-1am;)

Flor da Laranja

MOROCCAN €€

17 MAP P38, C2

Casablanca native Rabea Esserghini runs a one-woman show at the wonderful Flor da Laranja. Service is slow, but the cosy North African ambience and delicious Moroccan cuisine more than make up for it. Top picks include dolmas, mouth-watering couscous dishes, lamb, shrimp and vegie tagines,

Mercado da Ribeira

chicken with lemon confit, and
fresh berry crêpes for dessert.
(☏964 781 122; Rua da Rosa 206;
mains €14-16; ⏰7-11.30pm Mon-Sat;
🛜)

Alma   MODERN PORTUGUESE €€€

18 ❌ MAP P38, E5

Michelin-starred Henrique Sá Pessoa's flagship Alma is one of Portugal's destination restaurants and,
in our humble opinion, Lisbon's
best gourmet dining experience.
The casual space exudes under-
stated style amid the original stone
flooring and gorgeous hardwood
tables, but it's Pessoa's outra-
geously good nouveau Portuguese
cuisine that draws the foodie flock
from far and wide. (☏213 470 650;
www.almalisboa.pt; Rua Anchieta 15;
mains €29-33, tasting menus €80-100;
⏰noon-3pm & 7-11pm Tue-Sun; 🛜)

100 Maneiras   FUSION €€€

19 ❌ MAP P38, D2

How do we love 100 Maneiras?
Let us count the 100 ways... The
10-course tasting menu changes
twice yearly and features imaginative, delicately prepared dishes.
The courses are all a surprise –
part of the charm – though somewhat disappointingly, the chef will
only budge so far to accommodate
special diets and food allergies.
Reservations are essential for the
elegant and small space. (☏910
307 575; www.restaurante100maneiras.
com; Rua do Teixeira 35; tasting menu
€60, with classic/premium wine pairing
€95/120; ⏰7.30pm-2am; 🛜)

Mercado da Ribeira   👍

Doing trade in fresh fruit and
veg, fish and flowers since
1892, this domed **mar-
ket hall** (Map p38, C7; www.
timeoutmarket.com) has been
the word on everyone's lips
since *Time Out* transformed
half of it into a gourmet food
court in 2014. Now it's Lisbon
in chaotic culinary microcosm:
Garrafeira Nacional wines,
Café de São Bento steaks,
Manteigaria Silva cold cuts and
Michelin-star chef creations
from Henrique Sá Pessoa.

Drinking

Park   BAR

20 🍷 MAP P38, B4

If only all multistorey car parks
were like this... Take the elevator
to the 5th floor, and head up and
around to the top, which has been
transformed into one of Lisbon's
hippest rooftop bars, with sweeping views reaching right down
to the Rio Tejo and over the bell
towers of Igreja de Santa Catarina.
(www.facebook.com/parklisboaofficial;
Calçada do Combro 58; ⏰1pm-2am
Tue-Sat, to 8pm Sun; 🛜)

BA Wine Bar do Bairro Alto   WINE BAR

21 🍷 MAP P38, C3

Reserve ahead unless you want to
get shut out of Bairro Alto's best

Bairro Alto after Dark

For years, working-class Bairro Alto was the place to throw off your Salazar straitjacket and indulge in a little after-dark sleaze. But while call girls no longer prowl these alleyways, the libertine lives on: graffitied slums have morphed into shabby-chic boutiques, alternative arts venues, tiny bistros, bars and clubs. It's lacklustre and as dead as a disused theatre by day; come twilight the nocturnal hedonist rears its sleepy head. Lanterns are flicked on, shutters raised and taxi drivers hurtle through the grid of narrow lanes.

For the real spirit of Bairro Alto, take the lead of locals: move from one bar to the next as the mood and music takes you; head out onto the cobbles to toast new-found friendships with €1 beers; live for the night.

wine bar, where the genuinely welcoming staff will offer you three fantastic tasting choices based on your wine proclivities (wines from €5; tasting boards for one/four €13/47). The cheeses (from small artisanal producers) and charcuterie (melt-in-your-mouth black-pork *presuntos*) are not to be missed, either. Reservations are essential. (☏213 461 182; bawinebar@gmail.com; Rua da Rosa 107; ⏰6-11pm Tue-Sun; 📶)

Pavilhão Chinês   BAR

22 🚇 MAP P38, C1

Pavilhão Chinês is an old curiosity shop of a bar with oil paintings and model Spitfires dangling from the ceiling, and cabinets brimming with glittering Venetian masks and Action Men. Play pool or bag a comfy armchair to nurse a port or an exquisitely mixed classic cocktail (from €9.50). Prices are higher than elsewhere, but such classy kitsch doesn't come cheap. (www.facebook.com/pavilhaochineslisboa; Rua Dom Pedro V 89-91; ⏰6pm-2am)

Tasca Mastai   BAR

23 🚇 MAP P38, C4

This artsy, Italian-run bar-cafe is a refreshing change of pace for Bairro Alto – the long list of speciality Aperol Spritzes are worth the trip (try the tart and appley Hugo, summer-drink perfection in a glass). It's a small, corner spot, with old sewing tables and tightly spun corrugated-cardboard bar stools. Bruschettas help soak up all those cocktails. (www.facebook.com/tascadomastai; Rua da Rosa 14; ⏰3pm-midnight Tue-Fri, from 4pm Sat & Sun; 📶)

Duque Brewpub   PUB

24 🚇 MAP P38, E3

Lisbon's inaugural brewpub features 12 taps of Portuguese-only craft brews, a few of which are dedicated to on-site suds (under the banner of Cerveja Aroeira), brewed in true craft-beer style: no two batches are the same. Additional taps feature invitees such as Dois Corvos, Musa and Letra. (www.duquebrewpub.com; Duques da Calçada 49; ⏰4pm-midnight Sun-Wed, to 1am Thu, to 2am Fri & Sat; 📶)

O Bom O Mau e O Vilão

COCKTAIL BAR

25 🚇 MAP P38, D7

'The Good, the Bad and the Ugly' is an artsy drinking den sprung from a refurbished Pombaline town house. It's divided among several rooms draped in contemporary artworks and period furnishings. DJs throw down funk, soul, acid jazz and vintage beats to an eclectic, easy-on-the-eyes crowd that is mingle-friendly and more highbrow than average for the neighbourhood. (www.facebook.com/obomomaueovilao; Rua do Alecrim 21; ⏰7pm-2am Mon-Thu, to 3am Fri & Sat)

Loucos & Sonhadores

BAR

26 🚇 MAP P38, C2

This smoky, bohemian drinking den feels secreted away from the heaving masses on nearby streets. With kitschy decor, free (salty) popcorn and a wide range of tunes, it's a great place for eclectic conversation in the various rooms rather than taking shots. (Rua da Rosa 261; ⏰10pm-4am Mon-Sat)

Stupido 1/1

BAR

27 🚇 MAP P38, C6

More than just a bar for a casual drink, the hotspot in Cais do Sodré is an art installation curated by none other than street artist Vhils.

Drinks and live music are the only things that are fixed here; each year the decoration of the bar is changed by Vhils or artists he selects. (www.facebook.com/stupido.one; Rua de São Paulo 130; ⏰6pm-2am Tue-Thu, to 3am Fri & Sat, to 11.45pm Sun)

Noobai Café

BAR

28 🚇 MAP P38, B5

Great views, winning cocktails (€6 to €8.50) and a festive crowd make Noobai a popular draw for a sundowner at Miradouro de Santa Catarina.

The vibe is laid-back, the music is funky jazz and the views over the Rio Tejo are magical. (www.facebook.com/NoobaiPaginaOficial; Miradouro de Santa Catarina; ⏰10am-midnight)

Capela

BAR

29 🚇 MAP P38, D4

According to (questionable) legend this was once a Gothic chapel, but today Capela's gospel is an experimental line-up of electronica and funky house.

Get there early (before midnight) to appreciate the DJs before the crowds descend.

Frescoes, Renaissance-style nude murals and dusty chandeliers add a boho-chic touch. (www.facebook.com/acapelabar; Rua da Atalaia 45; ⏲8pm-2am Sun-Thu, to 3am Fri & Sat)

Discoteca Jamaica   CLUB

30 💀 MAP P38, D7

Gay and straight, Black and white, young and old – everyone has a soft spot for this offbeat club.

It gets going at around 2am on weekends with DJs pumping out reggae, hip hop and retro. (www.facebook.com/jamaicalisboa; Rua Nova do Carvalho 6; ⏲11.45pm-6am Tue-Sat)

Have Your Cake   🍴

Lisbon has one seriously sweet tooth and nearly every corner has a *pastelaria* (pastry shop).

Housed in a revamped butter factor, **Manteigaria** (Map p38, D5; www.facebook.com/manteigarialisboa; Rua do Loreto 2; pastel de nata €1; ⏲8am-midnight) hits the mark with its superb *pastéis de nata* – Portugal's classic crisp custard tarts.

For flawless chocolate cake, **Landeau** (Map p38, D6; www.landeau.pt; Rua das Flores 70; cake €3.70; ⏲noon-7pm; 📶) is unrivalled.

Entertainment

A Tasca do Chico   LIVE MUSIC

31 ⭐ MAP P38, D4

This crowded dive (reserve ahead), full of soccer banners and spilling over with people of all ilks, is a fado free-for-all. It's not uncommon for taxi drivers to roll up, hum a few bars, and hop right back into their cabs, speeding off into the night. (📞961 339 696; www.facebook.com/atasca.dochico; Rua do Diário de Notícias 39; ⏲noon-2am Sun-Thu, to 3am Fri & Sat)

Alface Hall   LIVE MUSIC

32 ⭐ MAP P38, D3

With one wall covered in LPs and another with old cinema chairs, there's an old-time feel to this jazz and blues bar in Bairro Alto. Free concerts happen nightly at 9.30pm on the minuscule stage (OK, it's just a spot on the floor). (www.facebook.com/alface.music.hall; Rua do Norte 96; ⏲4pm-midnight; 📶)

Fado in Chiado   LIVE MUSIC

33 ⭐ MAP P38, E4

Inside a small theatre, the 50-minute nightly shows here feature high-quality fado – a male and a female singer and two guitarists – and they're held early so you can grab dinner afterwards. (📞961 717 778; www.fadoinchiado.com; Espaço Chiado, Rua da Miséricordia 14; admission €18.50; ⏲7pm Mon-Sat)

MILOSK50/SHUTTERSTOCK ©

Teatro Nacional de São Carlos

Zé dos Bois
LIVE MUSIC

34 ⭐ MAP P38, D4

Focusing on tomorrow's performing arts and music trends, Zé dos Bois is an experimental venue with a graffitied courtyard and an eclectic line-up of theatre, film, visual arts and live music. (ZDB; www.zedosbois.org; Rua da Barroca 59; cover €6-10; ☺expositions 6-11pm Wed-Sat, concerts from 10pm)

Teatro Nacional de São Carlos
THEATRE

35 ⭐ MAP P38, E5

Teatro Nacional de São Carlos is worth visiting just to see the sublime gold-and-red interior (email ahead for €5 guided tours), but it also has opera, ballet and theatre seasons. The summer-time **Festival ao Largo** (www.festivalaolargo.pt; Largo de São Carlos; ☺late Jun-late Jul) features free outdoor concerts on the plaza facing the theatre (☎213 253 045; www.saocarlos.pt; Rua Serpa Pinto 9; ☺box office 1-7pm Mon-Fri)

Shopping

A Vida Portuguesa
GIFTS & SOUVENIRS

36 🔒 MAP P38, F5

A flashback to the late 19th century with its high ceilings and polished cabinets, this former warehouse and perfume factory lures nostalgics with its all-Portuguese products, from retro-wrapped Tricona sardines to Claus Porto soaps, and heart-embellished Viana do Castelo

Shop & Stroll on Rua do Carmo

Chiado's well-heeled Rua do Carmo is a catwalk to posh jewellers and designer names like Ana Salazar, while Rua Garrett is peppered with bookshops and speciality shops selling top-quality chocolate, coffee and more. For a more local scene, head to Rua Dom Pedro V and Príncipe Real, where you'll find the creations of up-and-coming Portuguese designers and antique, *azulejo* and interior design shops. Late-night shoppers hit Bairro Alto, where hole-in-the-wall boutiques and concept stores sell everything from vintage garb, glitzy club wear and limited-edition Adidas to cork art, ceramics and vinyl. Rua do Diário de Notícias, Rua das Salgadeiras and Rua do Norte are also worth a look.

embroideries to Bordalo Pinheiro porcelain swallows. There's also a location in **Intendente** (www.avidaportuguesa.com; Largo do Intendente 23; ☺10.30am-7.30pm). (www.avidaportuguesa.com; Rua Anchieta 11; ☺10am-8pm Mon-Sat, from 11am Sun)

Loja do Burel   CLOTHING

37 🔒 MAP P38, E5

Once a clothing staple of Serra da Estrela mountain-dwelling shepherds, Burel, a Portuguese black wool, was all but left to disappear until this company single-handedly resurrected the industry, giving it a stylish makeover fit for 21st-century fashion. The colourful blankets, handbags, jackets, hats and other home decor items aren't like anything anyone has back home. (www.burelfactory.com; Rua Serpa Pinto 15B; ☺10am-8pm Mon-Sat, 11am-7pm Sun)

Loja das Conservas   FOOD

38 🔒 MAP P38, E7

What appears to be a gallery is on closer inspection a fascinating temple to tinned fish (or *conservas* as the Portuguese say) – the result of an industry on its deathbed revived by a savvy marketing about-face and new generations of hipsters. The retro-wrapped tins, displayed along with the history of each canning factory, are artworks. (www.facebook.com/lojasconservas; Rua do Arsenal 130; ☺10am-8pm Mon-Sat, noon-9pm Sun)

Claus Porto   COSMETICS

39 🔒 MAP P38, D3

The amazing flagship store is in Porto, but Claus Porto, one of Portugal's most iconic brands, has its own evocative retro Lisbon boutique here as well. The painstakingly vintage art-deco and belle-époque-style packaging for the luxury soaps, lotions, room diffusers and notebooks are all original – resurrected from the brand's design archives. (www.clausporto.com/pt; Rua da Misericórdia 135; ⊘10am-9pm)

Apaixonarte DESIGN

40 🏢 MAP P38, A5

This corner design store sells only Portuguese-made home decor pieces and fashion accessories. Once a month the shop also welcomes art exhibits by local artists. Soaps, prints and small decoration items make popular souvenirs. (www.apaixonarte.com; Rua Poiais de São Bento 57; ⊘noon-7.30pm Mon-Fri, 11am-6pm Sat)

Cork & Company GIFTS & SOUVENIRS

41 🏢 MAP P38, D4

At this elegantly designed shop, you'll find cork put to surprisingly imaginative uses, with well-made and sustainable cork handbags, pens, wallets, journals, candleholders, hats, scarves, place mats, umbrellas, iPhone covers and even chaise longues! (www.corkandcompany.pt; Rua das

Salgadeiras 10; ⊘11am-7pm Mon-Sat, 5-7pm Sun)

Fábrica Sant'Ana ARTS & CRAFTS

42 🏢 MAP P38, D5

Handmaking and painting *azulejos* (from €5) since 1741, this is the place to get some eye-catching porcelain tiles for your home. (www.santanna.com.pt; Rua do Alecrím 95; ⊘9.30am-7pm Mon-Sat)

El Dorado VINTAGE, CLOTHING

43 🏢 MAP P38, D4

A gramophone plays vinyl classics as divas grab vintage styles from psychedelic prints to 6in platforms and pencil skirts at this Bairro Alto hipster place. There's also a great range of club wear. (📞213 423 935; Rua do Norte 23; ⊘1-9pm Mon-Thu, to 11pm Fri & Sat, 3-9pm Sun)

Livraria Bertrand BOOKS

44 🏢 MAP P38, E5

The world's oldest operating bookshop, open since 1732 according to *Guinness World Records,* Bertrand has excellent selections, including titles in English, French and Spanish. (📞213 476 122; www.bertrand.pt; Rua Garrett 73; ⊘9am-10pm Mon-Sat, 11am-8pm Sun)

Walking Tour 🥾

Strolling Príncipe Real

Príncipe Real, located between Bairro Alto and Rato, is an open-minded, bohemian neighbourhood, with markets, antique stores, boutiques and people-watching squares. This enclave is home to artists, up-and-coming designers and the gay community, giving it a creative, blissfully relaxed vibe.

Walk Facts

Start Esplanada Café;
🚌 202 or 758

End Cerveteca Lisboa;
🚌 202 or 758

Length 1.3km; 2 hours

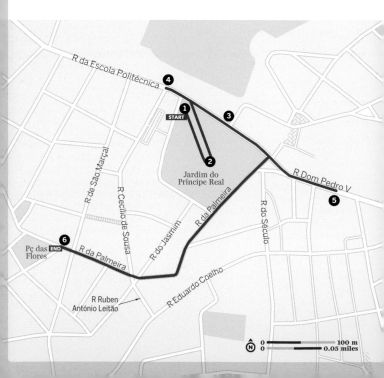

❶ Morning Coffee

Start your day in leisurely fashion at the **Esplanada Café** (www.facebook.com/esplanadadoprincipereal; Praça do Príncipe Real 23; mains €8-15, cocktails from €7; ☺9am-midnight Sun, Mon, Wed, to 5pm Tue, to 2am Thu-Sat; 🛜), a tree-shaded pit stop with tables under massive rubber tree palms.

❷ Plaza Stroll

A century-old cedar tree forms a giant natural parasol at the centre of palm-dotted **Jardim do Príncipe Real**, where *lisboêtas* from all walks of life hang out. The square is rimmed by elegant 19th-century town houses; most striking of all is the powder-puff-pink **Palacete Ribeiro da Cunha** at No 26.

❸ Innovative Design

If you want to find Lisbon's cutting edge, this neighbourhood is where it's at. Designers and creatives from the emerging to the established show their latest works at gorgeous concept stores like the neo-Moorish **Embaixada** (www.embaixadalx.pt; Praça do Príncipe Real 26; ☺noon-8pm Mon-Fri, 11am-7pm Sat & Sun, restaurants to 2am).

❹ Chocolate Wonderland

Make a re-fuelling stop at one of Lisbon's most cherished *chocolatarias*, **Bettina & Niccolò Corallo** (www.claudiocorallo.com; Rua da Escola Politécnica 4; chocolate per kg from €90; ☺11am-7pm Tue-Sat), a family-run transplant from São Tomé and Príncipe that does both exquisite chocolate and immensely satisfying coffee sourced from their family plantations in Africa.

❺ Fashion Focus

Lisbon is no longer the wallflower of the international fashion scene. The city has carved out a reputation as a catwalk capital to watch.Nowhere is this reflected more than on hip strip Rua Dom Pedro V, where you can check out Lidija Kolovrat's boldly patterned wonders at **Kolovrat** (www.lidijakolovrat.com; Rua Dom Pedro V 79; ☺11am-8pm Mon-Sat). Or see the nearby flagship store of clean-cut **Alexandra Moura** (www.alexandramoura.com; Praça do Príncipe Real 26, Embaixada, 2nd fl; ☺11am-8pm Mon-Sat).

❻ Craft-Beer Hideaway

For Lisbon's cosiest craft-beer bar, head down to the pretty and picturesque Praça das Flores, where **Cerveteca Lisboa** (www.cervetecalisboa.com; Praça das Flores 62; ☺3.30pm-1am Sun-Thu, to 2am Fri & Sat; 🛜) specialises in local suds along with choice international brews, painstakingly drink-tested by friendly owners Rui and Carolina. Sipping on a cold one in this pretty plaza – though not at the kiosk tables! – is a darn satisfying end-of-day exercise.

Explore ✦
Baixa & Rossio

Built high and mighty on the rubble of the 1755 earthquake, Baixa is Lisbon's riverfront gateway, its royal flag-bearer, its lifeblood. Trams rumble, buskers hold crowds captive and shoppers mill around old-world stores. The main drag, Rua Augusta, links the regal Praça do Comércio to Rossio, where you'll find a neighbourly vibe in closet-sized ginjinha (cherry liqueur) bars and street cafes.

○ **Núcleo Arqueológico da Rua dos Correeiros (p61)** Beholding layers of unearthed history deep in the fascinating Lisbon undergrowth at these Roman ruins.

○ **Igreja de São Domingos (p61)** Pondering hundreds of years of turmoil and destruction inside this ethereal 1241 sanctuary, Lisbon's most cinematic church.

○ **Ginjinha bars (p68)** Getting liquored up with the locals at sunset on shots of sour-cherry love around Largo de São Domingos.

○ **Arco da Rua Augusta (p57)** Taking in a bird's-eye view of the city's heart and soul, Praça do Comércio, from atop this triumphal arch built as a symbol of Lisbon's post-earthquake reconstruction.

Getting There & Around

Ⓜ Baixa-Chiado, Rossio, Terreiro do Paço, Restauradores stations.

🚊 Trams 12E (circular route) and 15E to Algés via Alcântara and Belém depart from Praça da Figueira. Trams 18E and 25E stop at Praça do Comércio; tram 18E en route to Ajuda via Alcântara; and tram 25E to Campo de Ourique via Estrela. Pick up tram 28E at Rua da Conceição or Martim Moniz.

Neighbourhood Map on p60

Elevador de Santa Justa (p64) TRABANTOS/SHUTTERSTOCK ©

Top Experience 📷

Stroll Through the Praça do Comércio

There's no place like Praça do Comércio for the 'wow, I'm in Lisbon!' effect. Everyone arriving by boat used to disembark here, and it still feels like the city's gateway, thronging with activity and trams. With its 18th-century arcades and triumphal arch, this is Lisbon at its monumental best. Wander the riverfront, gaze up at the equestrian statue, and witness the history of Lisbon mapped out in stone.

◉ MAP P60, C6

Terreiro do Paço

Arco da Rua Augusta

Built in the wake of the 1755 earthquake, this **triumphal arch** (Rua Augusta 2-10; admission €2.50; ⏰9am-9pm mid-May–Aug, shorter hours in winter) is a riot of columns crowned with allegorical figures representing Glory, Valour and Genius, and carried high by bigwigs including Vasco da Gama and Marquês de Pombal. A lift whisks you to the top, where fine views of Praça do Comércio, the river and the castle await.

Dom José I Statue

The square's centrepiece, an 18th-century equestrian statue of the king Dom José I, hints at the square's royal roots as the pre-earthquake site of Palácio da Ribeira.

Riverfront

Praça do Comércio leads elegantly down to the banks of the Rio Tejo. The riverfront promenade is a popular gathering spot, with its sweeping views, boat trips and buskers. Across the water you can glimpse the 110m-high Cristo Rei (p62).

ViniPortugal

Under the arcades, vaulted tasting room **ViniPortugal** (www.winesofportugal.info; Praça do Comércio; ⏰11am-7pm Apr-Oct, closed Sun Nov-Mar) is a viticultural organisation offering several wine tastings a day. A €3 enocard allows you to taste at least three Portuguese wines, from Alentejo whites to full-bodied Douro reds.

Pátio da Galé

Lisbon's showpiece, the Pátio da Galé, harbours the restored inner courtyard of the former royal palace. Following a huge makeover, the complex is home to the tourist office, Lisbon Shop (p69), and people-watching cafes and restaurants.

★ Top Tips

o Come in the early morning to appreciate the square at its most peaceful, and in the evening to see its monuments beautifully lit up.

o Tie in your visit with a tour – Praça do Comércio is the starting point for many boat excursions and city walks.

✕ Take a Break

Head to nearby **Fragoleto** (www.facebook.com/geladosfragoleto; Rua da Prata 61; small/medium/large €2.50/3.80/5.20; ⏰11am-8pm; 📶 📝) for rich, creamy Italian-style gelato, often in unusual flavours from ecologically sourced ingredients.

Quick and simple **Nova Pombalina** (www.facebook.com/anovapombalina; Rua do Comércio 2; sandwiches €3-4.50; ⏰7am-7.30pm Mon-Sat) slings delicious *leitão* (suckling pig) sandwiches to your plate (or to go) in 60 seconds or less.

Walking Tour 🚶

Baixa Back in Time

In the cobbled laneways of Baixa and Rossio, bee-yellow funiculars and trams rumble up steep inclines as they have since the late 19th century, shoeshiners ply their trade and speciality stores thrive. As you stroll, you will come across thimble-sized haberdasheries, old-world patisseries and cupboard-sized ginjinha bars that serve nostalgia in a shot glass.

Walk Facts

Start Azevedo Rua;
Ⓜ Rossio

End A Ginjinha; Ⓜ Rossio

Length 2.2km, 2 hours

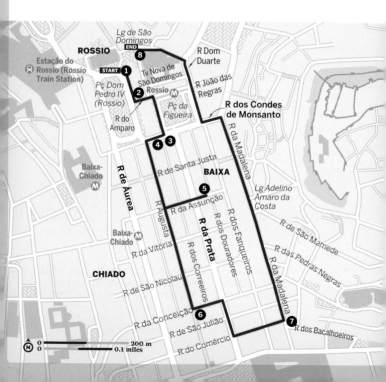

❶ Mad Hatters

Lisbon's maddest hatters, **Azevedo Rua** (☎ 213 470 817; www.azevedorua.pt; Praça Dom Pedro IV 73; ⏰ 9.30am-7.30pm Mon-Fri, 10am-2.30pm Sat) have been covering heads since 1886. Expect good old-fashioned service and wood-panelled cabinets full of tweedy flat caps, bonnets, straw hats, bowlers and Ascot-worthy headwear.

❷ Old-School Grocer

Shop grandma-style on Praça da Figueira and at century-old **Manteigaria Silva** (www.manteigariasilva.pt; Rua Dom Antão de Almada 1D; ⏰ 9am-7.30pm Mon-Sat), which does a brisk trade in ham, cheese, wine and *bacalhau* (dried salt-cod).

❸ Coffee & Cake

Since 1829 **Confeitaria Nacional** (www.confeitarianacional.com; Praça da Figueira 18; lunches €7-9; ⏰ 8am-8pm Mon-Thu, to 9pm Fri & Sat, 9am-9pm Sun) has been expanding waistlines with its egg and almond sweets, macaroons and *pastéis de nata* (custard tarts). Take a seat in the stuccoed interior for coffee and cake Lisbon-style.

❹ Portuguese Delicacies

As you make your way back towards Rossio, stop off at **Manuel Tavares** (www.manueltavares.com; Rua da Betesga 1A; ⏰ 9.30am-7.30pm Mon-Sat), a beautiful wood-fronted shop that has been tempting locals since 1860 with pata negra (cured ham), pungent cheeses, ginjinha and other treats.

❺ Vintage Valhalla

Vintage divas make for retro boutique **Outra Face da Lua** (www.facebook.com/aoutrafacedalua; Rua da Assunção 22; ⏰ 10am-7.30pm Mon-Sat; 🛜), crammed with puffball dresses, lurex skirts and wildly patterned '70s shirts. Jazz and electronica play overhead. Revive over light bites, cocktails and cosmic iced tea at the in-store cafe.

❻ Buttons & Threads

With its cluster of dark-wood-panelled, closet-sized haberdasheries, **Rua da Conceição** recalls an era where folk still used to darn stockings. Buttons, ribbons, threads and trimmings line the walls in art-nouveau **Retrosaria Bijou** (Rua da Conceição 91; ⏰ 9.30am-7pm Mon-Fri, to 1pm Sat) and many others like it.

❼ Retro Tinned Fish

How apt that in Rua dos Bacalhoeiros ('cod-vessel street') lies 1930s shop **Conserveira de Lisboa** (www.conserveiradelisboa.pt; Rua dos Bacalhoeiros 34; ⏰ 9am-7pm Mon-Sat), dedicated wholly to tinned fish, whose walls are a mosaic of retro wrappings. An elderly lady and her son tot up on a monstrous old till and wrap purchases in brown paper.

❽ Sundown Shots

Hipsters, old men in flat caps, office workers and tourists all meet at **A Ginjinha** (p68) for shots of cherry liqueur. Watch the owner line 'em up at the bar under the beady watch of the drink's 19th-century inventor, Espinheira.

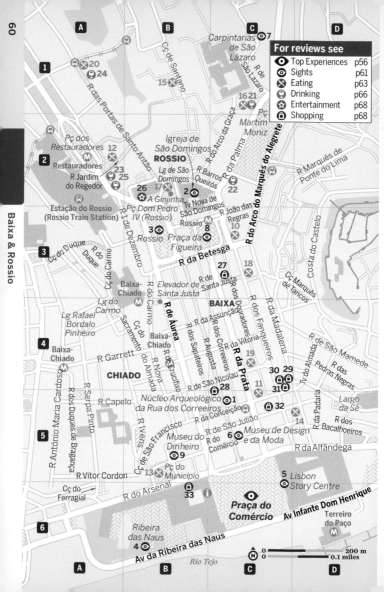

For reviews see

◉	Top Experiences	p56
◎	Sights	p61
🍴	Eating	p63
🍷	Drinking	p66
★	Entertainment	p68
🛍	Shopping	p68

Carpintarias de São Lázaro

Pç dos Restauradores

ROSSIO

Restauradores

R Jardim do Regedor

Igreja de São Domingos

Lg de São Domingos

A Ginjinha

Estação do Rossio (Rossio Train Station)

Pç Dom Pedro IV (Rossio)

Praça da Figueira

Tv Nova de São Domingos

Pç Martim Moniz

R da Betesga

Elevador de Santa Justa

Lg do Carmo

Lg Rafael Bordalo Pinheiro

BAIXA

Baixa-Chiado

CHIADO

R Garrett

Núcleo Arqueológico da Rua dos Correeiros

Museu do Dinheiro

Museu de Design e da Moda

Pç do Município

Cç do Ferragial

R do Arsenal

Praça do Comércio

Lisbon Story Centre

Terreiro do Paço

Ribeira das Naus

Av da Ribeira das Naus

Av Infante Dom Henrique

Rio Tejo

N 0   200 m
   0   0.1 miles

Sights

Núcleo Arqueológico da Rua dos Correeiros RUINS

1 ◉ MAP P60, C5

Hidden under the Millennium BCP bank building are layers of ruins dating from the Iron Age, discovered on a 1991 parking-lot dig. Book ahead for fascinating archaeologist-led tours, run by Fundação Millennium, that descend into the depths. In English or Portuguese departing on the hour and depending on bookings. (📞211 131 004; http://ind.millenniumbcp.pt; Rua Augusta 96; admission free; ⏱10am-6pm Mon-Sat)

Igreja de São Domingos CHURCH

2 ◉ MAP P60, B2

It's a miracle that this baroque church dating from 1241 still stands, having barely survived the 1755 earthquake, then fire in 1959. Its sea of tea lights illuminates gashed pillars, battered walls and ethereal sculptures in its musty yet enchanting interior. Note the Star of David memorial outside, marking the spot of a bloody anti-Semitic massacre in 1506. (www.patriarcado-lisboa.pt; Largo de São Domingos; admission free; ⏱7.30am-7pm)

Rossio PLAZA

3 ◉ MAP P60, B3

Simply known as Rossio to locals, Praça Dom Pedro IV has 24-hour buzz. Shoeshiners, lottery-ticket sellers, hash-peddlers and office workers drift across its wave-like cobbles, gazing up to its ornate fountains and **Dom Pedro IV** (Brazil's first emperor), perched high on a marble pedestal.

And these cobbles have seen it all: witch burnings and bullfights, rallies and 1974 revolution carnations. Don't miss **Estação do Rossio**, a frothy neo-Manueline station with horseshoe-shaped arches and swirly turrets. Trains depart here for Sintra. (Praça Dom Pedro IV)

Ribeira das Naus WATERFRONT

4 ◉ MAP P60, B6

This riverfront promenade between Praça do Comércio and Cais do Sodré is a focal point along Lisbon's continually regenerating waterfront. With broad views over the Rio Tejo, it's a fine place for strolling, lounging, reading, cycling or kicking back with a coffee at the kiosk. This is the closest Lisbon gets to an urban beach.

Lisbon Story Centre MUSEUM

5 ◉ MAP P60, C6

This museum takes visitors on a 60-minute journey through Lisbon's history, from its early foundation (pre-ancient Roman days) to modern times. An audio guide and multimedia exhibits describe key episodes, including New World discoveries, the terrifying 1755 earthquake (with a vivid film re-enacting the horrors) and the ambitious reconstruction that followed. (www.lisboastorycentre.pt; Praça do Comércio 78; adult/child €7/3; ⏱10am-8pm)

Cristo Rei

Visible from almost anywhere in Lisbon, the 110m **Cristo Rei** (www.cristorei.pt; Alto do Pragal, Av Cristo Rei, Almada; adult/child €5/2.50; ⏰9.30am-6.30pm 15 Jul-Aug, to 6pm Sep-Jun, to 6.45pm 1-15 Jul) is a statue of Christ with outstretched arms. The slightly more baroque version of Rio de Janeiro's *Christ the Redeemer* was erected in 1959 to thank God for sparing Portugal from the horrors of WWII. A lift zooms you up to a platform, and Lisbon spreads magnificently before you.

Museu de Design e da Moda   MUSEUM

6 ◉ MAP P60, C5

This Baixa star, set in a cavernous former bank, contains furniture, industrial design and couture dating from the 1930s. Highlights include iconic furniture by Charles Eames, Frank Gehry and Brazil's Campana Brothers; plus haute couture by the likes of Givenchy, Christian Dior and Balenciaga. (Mude; www.mude.pt; Rua Augusta 24; ⏰10am-6pm Tue-Sun)

Carpintarias de São Lázaro   CULTURAL CENTRE

7 ◉ MAP P60, C1

This cultural centre offers contemporary art exhibitions and more. Housed in a three-floor former carpenter's haunt, it survived a fire and years of neglect to become the new hub of contemporary art in the city, complete with restaurants, bars and lounge areas. (www.facebook.com/CarpintariasdeSaoLazaro; Rua de São Lázaro 72; admission free; ⏰3-7pm Wed-Sat)

Praça da Figueira   PLAZA

8 ◉ MAP P60, B3

Praça da Figueira is framed by whizzing traffic, Pombaline town houses and alfresco cafes with stellar views of hilltop Castelo de São Jorge. At its centre rises gallant **King João I**, once celebrated for his 15th-century discoveries in Africa, now targeted by pigeons and gravity-defying skateboarders.

Museu do Dinheiro   MUSEUM

9 ◉ MAP P60, B5

Pop into Banco do Portugal's money museum to see the stunning €34-million interior renovation of the once-mighty São Julião church (closed in 1933); and the more notable **Interpretation Centre for King Dinis' Wall**, a preserved 30m expanse of the 13th-century medieval city wall, located in the church's former crypt and discovered during a 2010 excavation. (www.museudodinheiro.pt; Largo de São Julião; admission free; ⏰10am-6pm Wed-Sat)

Eating

Eight Health Lounge
VEGAN €

10  MAP P60, C3

This refreshing Praça da Figueira spot is fiercely devoted to both plant-based sustenance and immaculate design. Clean-lined craft woodwork juxtaposed with industrial-sexy minimalism is the backbone of the gorgeous space, and a wildly tempting menu of fresh juices, smoothie bowls, panini, salads, toasts and wellness shots are given heightened attention to detail and flavour. (www.8healthlounge.com; Praça da Figueira 12A; mains €4.90-7.50; ☉9.30am-8pm Mon-Thu, to 3pm Fri, 11am-8pm Sun; ☎☏)

Pizzeria Romana al Taglio
PIZZA €

11  MAP P60, C5

This Roman transplant dishes out fresh and fast *pizza al taglio* – traditional, Roman-style pizza in square slices – in some 25 colourful and ridiculously inviting flavours, including at least a dozen vegan/veg options. Popular options such as *Cuor di Latte* (buffalo mozzarella, tomato, basil), *Diavola* (spicy salami) and *Boscaiola* (mushrooms and sausage) make for a great on-the-go meal while pounding Baixa's cobblestones. (www.romanapizza. it; Rua da Conceição 44; slices €1-4; ☉11.30am-10.30pm; ☏)

Baixa & Rossio Eating

Cristo Rei

HUGO FELIX/SHUTTERSTOCK ©

Grand Views from the Elevador de Santa Justa

If the lanky, wrought-iron **Elevador de Santa Justa** (Map p60, B4; cnrs Rua de Santa Justa & Largo do Carmo; www.carris.pt/en/elevators; ⏱7am-11pm Mar-Oct, to 9pm Nov-Feb) seems uncannily familiar, it's probably because the neo-Gothic marvel is the handiwork of Raul Mésnier, Gustave Eiffel's apprentice. It's Lisbon's only vertical street lift, built in 1902 and steam-powered until 1907. Get here early to beat the crowds and zoom to the top for sweeping views over the city's skyline.

Bear in mind, however, that some call the €5.15 fee Santa *Injusta!* You can save €3.50 by entering the platform from the top (behind Convento do Carmo via Bellalisa restaurant) and paying just €1.50 to access the viewing platform.

Pinóquio
PORTUGUESE €€

12 ✖ MAP P60, A2

Bustling Pinóquio is easy to miss as it's tucked into a *praça* corner partially obstructed by a souvenir kiosk. Dressed in white tablecloths against pea-green walls, it's distinctly old school, with indomitable waiters slinging a stunning slew of classic dishes like *arroz de pato* (duck rice), seafood *feijoada* and *arroz de bacalhau* (codfish rice). (☎213 465 106; www.restaurantepinoquio.pt; Praça dos Restauradores 79; mains €17-26; ⏱noon-midnight; 📶)

Delfina – Cantina Portuguesa
PORTUGUESE €€

13 ✖ MAP P60, B5

The restaurant at boutique hotel Alma Lusa embodies the spirit of typical Portuguese cuisine. The menu mixes staple dishes like *bacalhau à Brás* (shredded cod with onions, eggs and potatoes) with reinventions of traditional recipes that you'll find in the Delfina's Choices section, including an extensive and unconventional *açorda* menu. (☎212 697 445; www.almalusahotels.com/delfina; Praça do Município 21; mains €10-22; ⏱7.30am-midnight)

Tasca Kome
JAPANESE €€

14 ✖ MAP P60, D5

This blink-and-you'll-miss-it Japanese *tasca* is one of Lisbon's few turning out authentic cuisine from the Land of the Rising Sun. The menu doesn't overwhelm with options; instead, there's exquisite sushi, *tonkatsu* (breaded pork cutlets), *aji tataki* (horse mackerel with ginger and chives), *nasu dengaku* (fried eggplant with sweet miso) and daily-changing specials that bridge cultures (pork stew with daikon, for example). (☎211 340 117; www.kome-lisboa.com; Rua da Madalena 57; mains €8-23, sushi plates from €15; ⏱noon-2.30pm & 7-10pm Tue-Thu, noon-3pm & 7-10pm Fri, 12.30-3pm & 7-10pm Sat; 📶)

La Lupita Cozinha Tradicional Mexicana
MEXICAN €€

15 MAP P60, B1

Mexican City transplant Ramon and his Romanian wife run a free-style cafe called Casa do Campo during the week, but on Saturdays, Ramon whips out all his smuggled ingredients from the homeland for a real-deal Mexican brunch. (914 222 270; www.facebook.com/lalupitalisboa; Calçada de Santana 175; brunch €14; 11am-2pm Sat;)

Kin
ASIAN €€

16 MAP P60, C1

Topo's sexy Asian lounge – adjacent to their original rooftop location (p66) inside a Praça Martim Moniz commercial centre – is a Thai/Vietnamese/Indonesian/Chinese foursome under the watchful eye of a Chinese dragon figure draped overhead. Mostly Asian noodle and rice dishes (pad thai, nasi goreng) are paired with craft cocktails designed to complement the sweet and spice of the dishes. (www.topo-lisboa.pt; Centro Comercial Martim Moniz, 6th fl, Praça Martim Moniz; mains €10-14; 8-11pm Tue-Sat;)

Chaminés do Palácio
PORTUGUESE €€

17 MAP P60, B2

This 16th-century palace near Rossio square, a National Monument, goes unnoticed by most of the daily passers-by in the Baixa quarter. The restaurant inside serves home-made-style Portuguese cuisine in a casual and family-friendly atmosphere. Weather permitting, grab a table at the Arab-inspired interior courtyard with blue-and-white tiled walls. (www.chaminesdopalacio.pt; Largo de São Domingos 11, Palácio da Independência; mains €6.50-12.50; noon-3pm & 7-10pm Mon-Sat)

Less
PORTUGUESE €€

18 MAP P60, C3

With a view of Lisbon's landmarks, including the Santa Justa elevator and the Carmo Convent ruins, this rooftop bar and restaurant from chef Miguel Castro Silva makes use of the once-underappreciated top-floor of the kitchenware store Pollux – most folks not shopping for homewares walk right past it. (913 204 373; www.miguelcastrosilva.com; Rua dos Fanqueiros 276, 8th fl; mains €8.80-15.50; 10am-8pm Mon-Wed, to midnight Thu-Sat;)

Bebedouro
TAPAS €€

19 MAP P60, C4

Wine-bottle lights illuminate stylish Bebedouro, where full bodied Douro wines are nicely paired with tasting platters of regional cheese and sausage, creative salads and *petiscos* (tapas or small plates). The small, shotgun-style place has just five tables and five bar seats plus a little pavement terrace. (218 860 376; www.facebook.com/bebedourowineandfood; Rua de São Nicolau 24; tasting plates €17.70-39.50; noon-11.45pm Wed-Mon;)

Solar dos Presuntos

PORTUGUESE €€€

20 🍴 MAP P60, A1

Don't be fooled by the smoked *presunto* (ham) hanging in the window, this iconic restaurant is renowned for its excellent seafood too. Start with the excellent *pata negra* (cured ham), *paio* smoked sausage and cheese *couvert* (stew), then dig into a fantastic lobster *açorda,* delectable seafood paella or crustacean curry. (📞213 424 253; www.solardospresuntos.com; Rua das Portas de Santo Antão 150; mains €16-27.50, seafood per kg €29-98; ⏱12.30-3.30pm & 7-11pm Mon-Sat; 🛜)

Drinking

TOPO Martim Moniz

BAR

21 🍸 MAP P60, C1

This hipster hang-out is an excellent rooftop lounge with extraordinary views over lively Praça Martim Moniz and the whole of Lisbon. It features loungey open-air wooden benches for cocktails (€8 to €14), coffee and light bites, and a covered indoor lounge. It's all set to a vibey soundtrack, often courtesy of DJs. (www.topo-lisboa.pt; Centro Comercial Martim Moniz, 6th fl, Praça Martim Moniz; ⏱12.30pm-midnight Sun-Wed, to 1am Thu, to 2am Fri & Sat)

Hotel Mundial Rooftop Bar

BAR

22 🍸 MAP P60, C2

Grab a table at sundown on the Hotel Mundial's roof terrace for a sweeping view of Lisbon and its hilltop castle. The backlit bar, white sofas and ambient sounds set the stage for evening drinks and sharing plates. (www.hotel-mundial.pt; Praça Martim Moniz 2, Hotel Mundial; ⏱6.30-12.30pm Apr-Oct, to 11.30pm Nov-Mar)

O Bar da Odete

WINE BAR

23 🍸 MAP P60, A2

Saunter past the window strewn with Iberian pork legs to this intimate wine bar, where a dozen or two wines are served by the glass (€5 to €14) and paired with delicately sliced *presunto* (ham). Trust the staff's expert suggestions – all the wines here have been chosen by 'Odete Cascais', the pseudonym used by *Time Out Lisboa* – and the ham, mostly from Beira, is perfect. (www.facebook.com/OBardaOdete; Rua do Jardim do Regedor 47B; ⏱10am-midnight)

Fábrica Coffee Roasters

COFFEE

24 🍸 MAP P60, A1

Keep on walking past the touristy restaurants along pedestrianised Rua das Portas de Santo Antão to this sublime coffee temple, where serious caffeine is served amid a hodgepodge of exposed brick, hardwood floors and mismatched vintage furniture. Single-origin arabica beans from Brazil, Ethiopia and Colombia are roasted in-house and churned into distinctly third-wave cups of joe. Connoisseurs rejoice! (www.fabricacoffeeroasters.com; Rua das Portas de Santo Antão 136; ⏱9am-9pm)

The Earthquake that Shook Lisbon

The Fall of a Thriving City

Picture, if you can, Lisbon in its heyday: Portugal has discovered gold in Brazil; merchants are flocking to the city to trade in gold, spices, silks and jewels; the city is a magnificent canvas of 16th-century Manueline architecture. At the heart of it all is Baixa and the royal Palácio da Ribeira rising triumphantly above Terreiro do Paço square.

Now fast-forward to 9.40am on All Saints' Day, 1 November 1755: the day that everything changed. Three major earthquakes hit as residents celebrated Mass. The tremors brought an even more devastating fire and tsunami. Much of the city fell like a pack of dominoes, never to regain its former status; palaces, libraries, art galleries, churches and hospitals were razed to the ground. Some estimate that as many as 90,000 of Lisbon's 270,000 inhabitants died.

The Rise of Baixa & Pombaline Architecture

Enter the formidable, unflappable, geometrically minded Sebastião de Melo, better known as the Marquês de Pombal. As Dom João I's chief minister, the Marquês de Pombal swiftly set about reconstructing the city, good to his word to 'bury the dead and heal the living'. In the wake of the disaster, the autocratic statesman not only kept the country's head above water as it was plunged into economic chaos, but he also managed to propel Lisbon into the modern era.

Together with military engineers and architects Eugenio dos Santos and Manuel da Maia, the Marquês de Pombal played a pivotal role in reconstructing the city in a simple, cheap, earthquake-proof way that created today's formal grid, and Pombaline style was born. The antithesis of rococo, Pombaline architecture was functional and restrained: azulejos (hand-painted tiles) and decorative elements were used sparingly, building materials were prefabricated, and wide streets and broad plazas were preferred.

The best example of Pombaline style is the Baixa Pombalina, delineated by Rossio to the north and Praça do Comércio to the south. The neighbourhood has been on the Unesco list of tentative World Heritage Sites since 2004.

Bar Rossio

BAR

25 MAP P60, A2

A terrific rooftop spot for an afternoon coffee or drinks (cocktails from €9 to €17) as the city lights begin to glow. (www.altishotels.com; Altis Avenida Hotel, Rua 1 Dezembro 120; 7am-midnight;)

Ginjinha Bars

Come dusk, the area around Largo de São Domingos and Rua das Portas de Santo Antão buzzes with locals getting their cherry fix in a cluster of *ginjinha* bars. **A Ginjinha** (Map p60, B2; Largo de Saõ Domingos 8; ⏲9am-10pm) is famous as the birthplace of the sugary sweet tipple thanks to a quaffing friar from Igreja Santo Antonio who revealed the secret to an entre-preneurial Galician by the name of Espinheira. Nearby are other postage-stamp-sized bars to try. For little more than €1, your *ginjinha* can be ordered *sem* (without) or – our favourite – *com* (with) the alcohol-soaked cherries. It's a fine way to start or end your evening.

Entertainment

Teatro Nacional de Dona Maria II THEATRE

26 ⭐ MAP P60, B2

Rossio's graceful neoclassical theatre has a somewhat hit-and-miss schedule due to underfunding. Guided tours are at 11am Mondays (not August). The theatre's gran-deur evokes nothing of its sinister background as Palácio dos Estaus, seat of the Portuguese Inquisition from 1540. (📞800 213 250; www.teatro-dmaria.pt; Praça Dom Pedro IV; ⏲box office 11am-10pm Wed-Fri, 2-10pm Sat, 10.30am-7pm Tue & Sun)

Shopping

Garrafeira Nacional WINE

27 🏠 MAP P60, C3

This Lisbon landmark has been selling Portuguese juice since 1927 and is easily the best spot to pick up a bevy of local wines and spirits. Be steered towards lesser-known boutique wines and vintage ports in addition to the usual suspects. The small museum features vintages dating to the 18th century. (📞218 879 080; www.garrafeiranacional.com; Rua de Santa Justa 18; ⏲9.30am-7.30pm Mon-Fri, to 7pm Sat)

Typographia CLOTHING

28 🏠 MAP P60, C5

With shops in Porto and Madrid as well, this T-shirt shop is one of Europe's best. It features a select, monthly-changing array of clever, locally designed T-shirts (€23.95), which no one else will be wearing back home. (www.typographia.com; Rua Augusta 93; ⏲10am-7pm)

Santos Ofícios ARTS & CRAFTS

29 🏠 MAP P60, C4

If you have always fancied a hand-embroidered fado shawl, check out this brick-vaulted store. A must-shop for Portuguese folk art, including Madeira lace, *barro negro* glazed earthenware and miniature matchstick art from André Monteiro, among other high-quality, non-kitschy wares. (www.santosoficios-artesanato.pt; Rua da Madalena 87; ⏲10am-7.30pm Mon-Sat)

A Ginjinha

Soma Ideas   ARTS & CRAFTS

30 MAP P60, C4

Traditional Portuguese imagery gets a modern, design-forward twist at this not-so-average souvenir shop. Colourful coffee mugs, ceramics and framed art dominate – and you won't regret your purchases a year later! (www.somaideas.com; Rua dos Fanqueiros 98/100; ⏰10am-8.30pm)

Queijaria Nacional   FOOD

31 MAP P60, C4

A one-stop cheese shop with varieties from all over Portugal – from pungent and creamy Serra da Estrela offerings to Azores and Alentejo varieties. You can also pair cheese and charcuterie with Portuguese wines during a tasting here. (Rua da Conceição 8; ⏰10am-7pm)

Espaço Açores   FOOD

32 MAP P60, C5

The closest you can get to actually visiting the Azores in Lisbon is this attractive shop, where a taste of the islands comes in the form of cheeses, honeys, preserves, liqueurs and, apparently, the oldest tea produced in Europe. (www.espacoacores.pt; Rua de São Julião 58; ⏰10am-2pm & 3-7pm Mon-Sat)

Lisbon Shop   GIFTS & SOUVENIRS

33 MAP P60, B6

Housed in the Pombaline Pátio da Galé complex, this shop is crammed with Portuguese gifts. It's run by Ask Me Lisboa, the public face of Lisbon tourism. (www.askmelisboa.com; Rua do Arsenal 15; ⏰9.30am-7.30pm)

Walking Tour 🥾

Baixa to Santa Catarina

Shopping in Baixa's old-world stores, culture in Chiado's museums, captivating sunset views from Santa Catarina – it's all packed into this 'greatest hits' tour of downtown Lisbon. This afternoon walk gives you a palpable sense of Lisbon's history – on Baixa's regal plazas, in Pombaline backstreets built in the wake of the 1755 earthquake, and in literary-flavoured cafes, where poets like Fernando Pessoa once hung out.

Walk Facts

Start Praça do Comércio;
Ⓜ Terreiro do Paço

End Santa Catarina;
🚋 28E

Length 4.5km; 3½ hours

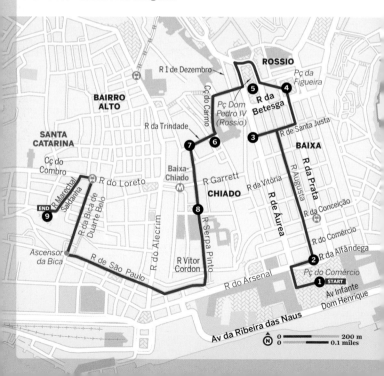

❶ Praça do Comércio

At Lisbon's riverside gateway, **Praça do Comércio** (p56), trams rumble past palatial facades, arcades and a gallant equestrian statue of Dom José I. Nip into **ViniPortugal** (p57) to taste Portuguese wines for €2.

❷ Rua Augusta

Pass through the triumphal **Arco da Rua Augusta** (p57) onto the main thoroughfare, Rua Augusta, buzzing with street entertainers and shoppers. From here, explore backstreets like old-fashioned **Rua da Conceição**.

❸ Elevador de Santa Justa

When you hit Rua de Santa Justa, swing left for the neo-Gothic **Elevador de Santa Justa** (p64), Lisbon's only vertical street lift. Enjoy 360-degree views from the viewing platform.

❹ Praça da Figueira

Saunter east along Rua de Santa Justa then north up Rua da Prata to **Praça da Figueira** (p62) for castle views from below. The square is rimmed with cafes and old-school stores.

❺ Rossio

Head straight onto **Rossio** (p61), one of Lisbon's grandest squares with its wave-like cobbles, fountains, neoclassical theatre and neo-Manueline Estação do Rossio.

❻ Largo do Carmo

Past the train station, Calçada do Carmo climbs to Chiado's **Largo do Carmo**, where jacaranda trees shade pavement cafes and the 18th-century Chafariz do Carmo fountain. Rising above it are the ethereal arches of the ruined **Convento do Carmo** (p34).

❼ Casa do Ferreira das Tabuletas

Cross the square to Rua da Trindade and the 1864 **Casa do Ferreira das Tabuletas**, where the trompe l'œil *azulejos* (handpainted tiles) depict allegorical figures and the elements.

❽ Rua Serpa Pinto

Follow the road south, past the 18th-century opera house **Teatro Nacional de São Carlos** (p49). Further on is modern art gallery **Museu do Chiado** (p40).

❾ Santa Catarina

Turn right and follow the trams along elegant Rua de São Paulo for a ride on the 1892 **Ascensor da Bica** (p41). Descend Rua Marechal Saldanha to **Miradouro de Santa Catarina** (p40) for sunset views of the river.

Worth a Trip 🔭

Trundle along on
Scenic Tram 28E

There's a reason why tram 28E tops most travellers' Lisbon wishlists. This rickety, screechy, gloriously old-fashioned ride between Praça Martim Moniz and Campo de Ourique provides 45 minutes of mood-lifting views and absurdly steep climbs. Use your powers of persuasion to bag a space by the window and prepare for a self-guided city tour to remember.

www.carris.pt/en/
tram/28E

€2.90 onboard fare

Graça

The grocery stores, wrought-iron lanterns and washing-strewn town houses seem, at times, close enough to touch as the tram scoots along the narrow, curving backstreets of Graça. Keep your eyes out for the graceful twin spires of **Igreja de São Vicente de Fora**.

Castelo & Alfama

As the tram descends, try to sit on the left side of the carriage for fleeting views across Alfama's mosaic of red rooftops to the Rio Tejo and close-ups of **Sé** (cathedral). Jump off at **Largo das Portas do Sol** for an incredible city panorama, or make the short climb up to **Castelo de São Jorge**. Tram-surfers are often spotted clinging perilously to the doors to dodge paying for a ticket.

Baixa & Chiado

Settle back as you rumble through the Pomba-line streets of Baixa and then begin the ascent to the elegant, mosaic-tiled **Praça Luís de Camões**, centred on a statue of its eponymous poet. As the tram climbs higher towards Estrela there are great snapshot views of the city and river.

Estrela & Prazeres

As the tram continues past *azulejo*-tiled and pastel-hued facades on the Calçada da Estrela, the neoclassical **Palácio da Assembleia da República** as **Basílica da Estrela** slide into view. Stay right until the end (Campo de Ourique) for a stroll around **Cemitério dos Prazeres**, built in 1833, dotted with monumental tombs and commanding views down to the river and Ponte 25 de Abril.

★ Top Tips

o Mind your personal belongings – tram 28E is fertile ground for pickpockets.

o Your best bet for snagging a seat is entering the tram at the beginning or end of the route (Martim Moniz or Campo de Ourique).

o Want to hop on and off at your leisure? Invest in a 24-hour Carris pass (€6.30), which covers all trams and funiculars.

o Among the city's other attractive tram rides are tram 12E from Praça da Figueira through the narrow streets of Alfama; tram 18E from Rua Alfândega to the Palácio da Ajuda via Alcântara; and tram 15E from Praça da Figueira.

✕ Take a Break

One of Lisbon's best craft breweries, 8ª Colina, has opened the beer kiosk Quiosque 8ª Colina (p88) on Largo da Graça – the perfect stop for a cold one along the tram route.

Explore ✦
Alfama, Castelo & Graça

This is the Lisbon you have no doubt dreamed about: a Moorish castle slung on a hillside, cobbled alleys twisting to sky-high viewpoints and laundry-strung houses in a fresco-painter's palette of colours. In this corner of the city, life is played out on the streets. Fado still rocks as it did way back when, one-pan family bistros fire up their grills at lunchtime, and the neighbourly vibe keeps things alluringly low-key.

○ **Alfama (p78)** Wandering the labyrinthine lanes of this Moorish time capsule, Lisbon's most atmospheric neighbourhood.

○ **Castelo de São Jorge (p76)** Roaming the ramparts of these mid-11th-century hilltop fortifications.

○ **Largo das Portas do Sol (p79)** Kicking back with a coffee or cocktail with the best views of the rust-shaded jumble of rooftops over Alfama.

○ **Museu do Aljube (p82)** Contemplating the haunting reality of life under Europe's longest dictatorship at this museum inside a former political prison.

Getting There & Around

🚋 Tram 28E bowls through Castelo and Graça. Key stops: Largo das Portas do Sol, Sé and Largo da Graça.

Ⓜ The blue line to Santa Apolónia is a quick way of reaching the sights closest to the river.

🚌 Take the 734 from Martim Moniz to Santa Apolónia train station for Largo da Graça and Campo de Santa Clara.

Neighbourhood Map on p80

Top Experience 📷
Explore History at the Castelo de São Jorge

Gazing grandly over the city, these heavily restored hilltop fortifications evoke Lisbon's history from the bold to the bloody. The castle dates to the mid-11th century when the Moors ruled Lisbon and the stronghold was the heart of their alcáçova (citadel). Christian crusaders, royals and convicts; battles, coronations and an earthquake – this castle has seen it all.

◎ MAP P80, B3

www.castelodesaojorge.pt

adult/student/child
€8.50/5/free

🕘9am-9pm Mar-Oct,
to 6pm Nov-Feb

Ramparts & Garden

Shaded by pine trees, the castle's ramparts afford far-reaching views over Lisbon. From here you can glimpse the river and Ponte 25 de Abril, contrast the grid-like streets of Baixa with the high-rises of the modern districts, and pick out the city's monuments and plazas. Peacocks strut proudly through the adjacent gardens, littered with ruins.

Tower of Ulysses & Periscope

Of all the castle's 11 towers, the Tower of Ulysses has the most gripping history. It once housed the royal treasury and archives, and was nicknamed the Torre do Tombo (Tumbling Tower) because the most important things in the kingdom used to 'tumble' into it. It now contains a periscope, or camera obscura, which gives a 360-degree view of the city in real time.

Núcleo Museológico

This museum makes a fair stab at drawing together the different epochs of the castle's history (and prehistory) and spelling them out in artefacts. On display is the fruit of archaeological digs – fragments of Iron Age pottery, Roman wine vessels, medieval oil lamps and coins, 17th-century *azulejos* (hand-painted tiles) and the like.

Archaeological Site

OK, it's time to use your imagination to piece together the parts of the castle's past with a wander around this archaeological site. In a quiet corner of the fortress, you can just about make out where the first settlement was in the 7th century BC, the remains of the mid-11th-century Moorish dwellings and the ruins of the last royal residence, destroyed in the 1755 earthquake.

★ **Top Tips**

o Join one of the free 1½-hour guided tours of the castle at 10.30am, 1pm and 4pm daily. Free 20-minute tours of the Tower of Ulysses run every 20 minutes.

o Pick up a free map and guide at the entrance.

o Arrive early or late in the day for fewer crowds.

o Come back at dusk for perfect snapshots of the illuminated castle.

✗ **Take a Break**

Follow the scent of chargrilled fish to local favourite **Páteo 13** (www.facebook.com/pateo13; Calçadinha de Santo Estêvão 13; mains €7.50-9.50; ⏱ noon-10pm Tue-Thu, to 11pm Fri-Sun, closed Nov Feb; 🛜), tucked away on a small, festively decorated plaza in Alfama.

Alfama, Castelo & Graça Explore History at the Castelo de São Jorge

Walking Tour 🥾

Alfama Backstreets

Alfama and its neighbours, Graça and Castelo, afford snapshots of daily life on flower-draped squares, at weekend flea markets, and in hidden alleys full of unexpected beauty and banter.

Walk Facts

Start Miradouro de Santa Luzia; 🚋 28E

End Miradouro da Senhora do Monte; 🚋 28E

Length 5km; 2–3 hours

❶ River Gazing

Views across Alfama's rooftops to the Rio Tejo beckon from the bougainvillea-wreathed **Miradouro de Santa Luzia** (Largo Santa Luzia) on Rua do Limoeiro. At the back, note the blue-and-white *azulejo* tile panels depicting scenes from the Siege of Lisbon in 1147 and the early-18th-century Praça do Comércio.

❷ Castelo's Side Streets

Few explore the atmospheric web of lanes around Castelo de São Jorge, such as **Rua Santa Cruz do Castelo**, studded with pastel-hued houses, hole-in-the-wall bars and grocers. Slow the pace here for a sense of the old Moorish *alcáçova*, once home to the city's elite.

❸ Moorish Gateway

The Moorish gateway **Largo das Portas do Sol** has postcard views of Alfama and Graça. Peer across a mosaic of red rooftops to the Panteão Nacional's ivory-white dome and twin-spired Igreja de São Vicente de Fora.

❹ Hidden Azulejos

Following the tram tracks downhill brings you to **Sé** (p83), Lisbon's imposing Gothic cathedral. Behind it is **Rua de São João da Praça**, with vaulted cafes, fado clubs and *azulejo*-clad facades – look for diamond-tip patterns at No 88 and floral motifs at No 106.

❺ Alfama Stroll

At Alfama's higgledy-piggledy heart is **Largo de São Miguel**, identified by its twin-towered chapel and palm tree, and **Rua dos Remédios**, perfect for a mooch with its cafes, grocery stores and galleries. In alleys close by, melancholic fado drifts from open windows, men play backgammon, chefs grill sardines and neighbours trade gossip just as they have for centuries.

❻ Flea-Market Finds

To see Graça at its lively best, visit on Tuesday or Saturday when **Campo de Santa Clara** becomes the giant **Feira da Ladra** (p91) (flea market), with locals gathering to sell tat and treasures in the shadow of the gracefully domed Panteão Nacional.

❼ Summertime Hang-Out

A much-loved summertime hang-out of *lisboêtas* is **Miradouro da Graça** (Largo da Graça). This terrace, near the baroque Igreja da Graça, has an incredible vista to the castle sitting plump on the hillside, the river and the Ponte 25 de Abril. Sunset is prime-time viewing.

❽ Lisbon's Highest Viewpoint

For a top-of-the-city view, huff up to **Miradouro da Senhora do Monte** (Rua da Senhora do Monte), one of the lesser-known *miradouros* in Lisbon, despite being the highest. From this pine-shaded plaza, the entire city spreads out picturesquely before you.

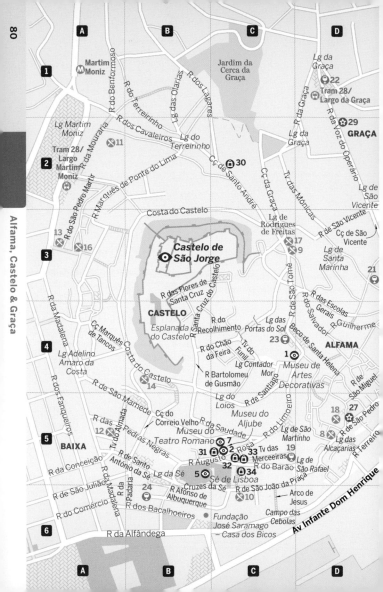

A **B** **C** **D**

1

Ⓜ Martim Moniz

R do Benformoso

R do Terreirinho

R das Olarias

R dos Lagares

Jardim da Cerca da Graça

Lg da Graça

Ⓧ 22
Tram 28/ Largo da Graça

R da Graça

R da Voz do Operário

⊛ 29 **GRAÇA**

2

Lg Martim Moniz

Tram 28/ Largo Martim Moniz

R da Mouraria

R dos Cavaleiros

Lg do Terreirinho

Ⓧ 11

R Marquês de Ponte do Lima

Cç de Santo André

🔒 30

Cç da Graça

Lg da Graça

Tv das Mónicas

Lg de São Vicente

R de São Vicente

Cç de São Vicente

3

R do São Pedro Mártir

Ⓧ 13

Ⓧ 16

Costa do Castelo

⊙ **Castelo de São Jorge**

Lg de Rodrigues de Freitas

Ⓧ 17
Ⓧ 9

R de São Tomé

Lg de Santa Marinha

Ⓧ 21

4

R da Madalena

Cç Marquês de Tancos

Costa do Castelo

R das Flores de Santa Cruz do Castelo

CASTELO

Esplanada do Castelo

Santa Cruz do Castelo

R do Recolhimento

Lg das Portas do Sol

Ⓧ 23

R das Escolas Gerais

R do Salvador

R Guilherme

Beco de Santa Helena

ALFAMA

R de São Miguel

5

Lg Adelino Amaro da Costa

R dos Fanqueiros

R de São Mamede

Cç do Castelo

Ⓧ 14

R do Chão da Feira

R Contador Mor

R Bartolomeu de Gusmão

Tv do Funil

◉ 1
Museu de Artes Decorativas

Ⓧ 18
⊛ 27

R de São Pedro

BAIXA

R das Pedras Negras

Ⓧ 12

Cç do Correio Velho

R da Amada

Tv de Santo António da Sé

R de Santo António da Sé

Museu do Aljube

Museu do Teatro Romano

◉ 7
Ⓧ 2
🔒 31

Lg dos Loios

R de Santiago

R da Saudade

R do Limoeiro

Lg de São Martinho

R da Rosa

19

Ⓧ 8

Lg das Alcaçarias

R Terreiro

6

R de São Julião

R da Conceição

R da Padaria

R da Madalena

Ⓧ 24

R Augusto

🔒 32

Lg da Sé

Ⓧ 5

Sé de Lisboa

Cruzes da Sé

R Afonso de Albuquerque

R dos Bacalhoeiros

R do Comércio

R da Alfândega

🔒 33
🔒 34

Tv das Merceeiras

R do Barão

Lg de São Rafael

Ⓧ 10

R de São João da Praça

Arco de Jesus

Campo das Cebolas

Fundação José Saramago – Casa dos Bicos

Av Infante Dom Henrique

A **B** **C** **D**

Alfama, Castelo & Graça

For reviews see

👁	Top Experiences	p76
⊙	Sights	p82
✖	Eating	p84
🍷	Drinking	p87
★	Entertainment	p89
🛍	Shopping	p90

Campo de Santa Clara

Campo de Santa Clara

Arco Grande da Cima

15

35

Panteão Nacional **6**

Cais de Pedra à Bica do Sapato

20

4

Mosteiro de São Vicente de Fora

Lg do Outeirinho da Amendoeira

R do Paraíso

Santa Apolónia Train Station

Ti-Natércia

Santa Apolónia Ⓜ

R dos Corvos

28 **26** **25**

R do Vigário

R do Museu de Artilharia

Calçadinha de Santo Estêvão

R dos Remédios

Av Infante Dom Henrique

R do Jardim do Tabaco

Cais de Pedra à Bica do Sapato

Lg do Chafariz de Dentro

do Trigo

3

Museu do Fado

Doca do Jardim do Tabaco

Rio Tejo

Ⓝ 0 ———————————— 400 m
0 ———————————— 0.2 miles

Sights

Museu de Artes Decorativas

MUSEUM

1  MAP P80, C4

Set in a petite 17th-century palace, the Museu de Artes Decorativas creaks under the weight of treasures including blingy French silverware, priceless Qing vases and Indo-Chinese furniture, a collection amassed by a wealthy Portuguese banker from the age of 16. It's worth a visit alone to admire the lavish apartments, embellished with baroque *azulejos,* frescoes and chandeliers. (Museum of Decorative Arts; www.fress.pt; Largo das Portas do Sol 2; adult/child €4/free; ☺10am-5pm Wed-Mon)

Museu do Aljube

MUSEUM

2  MAP P80, C5

Both poignant and haunting, this highly important museum has turned the former Portuguese dictatorship's political prison of choice into a museum of truth and consequence, memorial and remembrance – it's a must-see. Disturbing tales of authoritarian dictatorship are found over three floors (beginning with the *Ditadura Militar* in 1926, and evolving into the *Estado Novo*, or New State, from 1933 to 1974), including those of government torture, eaves-dropping, oppression, coercion, informing and censorship. (www.museudoaljube.pt; Rua de Augusto Rosa 42; adult/child €3/free; ☺10am-6pm Tue-Sun, free Sun until 2pm)

Sé de Lisboa

TTSTUDIO/SHUTTERSTOCK ©

Museu do Fado   MUSEUM

3 📍 MAP P80, E5

Fado (traditional Portuguese melancholic song) was born in Alfama. Immerse yourself in its bittersweet symphonies at Museu do Fado. This engaging museum traces fado's history from its working-class roots to international stardom. (www.museudofado.pt; Largo do Chafariz de Dentro; adult/child €5/3; ⏲10am-6pm Tue-Sun)

Mosteiro de São Vicente de Fora   CHURCH

4 📍 MAP P80, E3

Graça's Mosteiro de São Vicente de Fora was founded in 1147 and revamped by Italian architect Felipe Terzi in the late 16th century. Since the adjacent church took the brunt of the 1755 earthquake (the church's dome crashed through the ceiling of the **sacristy**, but emerged otherwise unscathed), elaborate blue-and-white *azulejos* dance across almost every wall, echoing the building's architectural curves. (Largo de São Vicente; adult/child €5/free; ⏲10am-6pm Tue-Sun)

Sé de Lisboa   CATHEDRAL

5 📍 MAP P80, B5

The fortress-like Sé de Lisboa is one of Lisbon's icons, built in 1150 on the site of a mosque soon after Christians recaptured the city from the Moors. It was sensitively restored in the 1930s. Despite the masses outside, the rib-vaulted interior, lit by a rose window, is calm. Stroll around the cathedral to spy leering gargoyles above the orange trees. (Largo de Sé; admission free; ⏲9am-7pm Tue-Sat, to 5pm Sun & Mon)

José Saramago Foundation

The Casa dos Bicos houses the **Fundação José Saramago** (Map p80, B6; www.josesaramago.org; Rua dos Bacalhoeiros 10; adult/child €3/free; ⏲10am-6pm Mon-Sat), with a small museum dedicated to Portugal's most famous writer, and a ground-floor excavation of Roman ruins. Opposite stands an olive tree, where Saramago's ashes were scattered in 2011. With its historic resonance and location close to the river, there could not be a more fitting tribute than this 16th-century landmark for the country's literary heavyweight.

Panteão Nacional   MUSEUM

6 📍 MAP P80, F2

Perched high and mighty above Graça's Campo de Santa Clara, the porcelain-white Panteão Nacional is a baroque beauty. Originally intended as a church, it now pays homage to Portugal's heroes and heroines, including 15th-century explorer Vasco da Gama and *fadista* (fado singer) Amália Rodrigues. (www.panteaonacional.gov.pt; Campo de Santa Clara; adult/child €4; ⏲10am-6pm Tue-Sun, to 5pm Oct-Mar)

Museu do Teatro Romano
MUSEUM

7 ⊙ MAP P80, C5

The ultramodern Museu do Teatro Romano catapults you back to Emperor Augustus' rule in Olisipo (Lisbon). The star attraction is a ruined **Roman theatre**, extended in AD 57, buried in the 1755 earthquake and finally unearthed in 1964. (Roman Theatre Museum; www.museudelisboa.pt; Rua de São Mamede 3A; adult/child €3/free; ☉10am-6pm Tue-Sun, free Sun until 2pm)

Eating

Medrosa d'Alfama
CAFE €

8 ✕ MAP P80, D5

This friendly cafe has a handful of tables on one of Alfama's prettiest squares. It's a fine spot for a craft beer with grilled chorizo, *tibornos* (Portuguese-style bruschetta), a €2.50 glass of sangria or a quick caffeine jolt. (www.medrosadalfama.pt; Largo de São Rafael 6; small plates €3.50-10; ☉noon-midnight Wed-Mon; 🛜🖉)

Marcelino Pão e Vinho
PORTUGUESE €

9 ✕ MAP P80, C3

What this narrow cafe lacks in space it makes up for in atmosphere, with local artworks on the walls, occasional live music, traditional hats suspended from the ceiling and wine-crate-lined walls. It's a cosy spot for refreshing sangria, and salads, sandwiches and tapas, including a fun meat grill

flamed up tableside in traditional crockware. (Rua do Salvador 62; mains €4-9; ☉10am-2am Thu-Tue; 🛜)

Pois Café
CAFE €

10 ✕ MAP P80, C6

Boasting a laid-back vibe under dominant stone arches, atmospheric Pois Café has creative salads, sandwiches and fresh juices, plus a handful of heartier daily specials. Its sofas invite lazy afternoons spent reading novels and sipping coffee, but you'll fight for space with the laptop brigade. (www.poiscafe.com; Rua de São João da Praça 93; mains €7-10; ☉noon-11pm Mon, 10am-11pm Tue-Sun; 🛜)

O Zé da Mouraria
PORTUGUESE €€

11 ✕ MAP P80, A2

Don't be fooled by the saloon-like doors, there's a typical Portuguese *tasca* inside: homey local cuisine, blue-and-white-tiled walls, chequered tablecloths – and it's one of Lisbon's best. The house-baked cod loaded with chickpeas, onions, garlic and olive oil is rightfully popular, and daily specials make return trips tempting. Service is a lost cause. (📞218 865 436; Rua João do Outeiro 24; mains for 2 €16.50-33.50; ☉noon-4pm Mon-Sat; 🛜)

Prado
PORTUGUESE €€

12 ✕ MAP P80, A5

This all-organic small-plates spot comes courtesy of Chef António Galapito, after his stint at Taberna do Mercado (Michelin-star chef

SALVADOR AZNAR/SHUTTERSTOCK ©

Nuno Mendes' Portuguese restaurant in London). Beautifully presented plates explode with fresh, clean flavours and change daily. (☏ 210 534 649; www.pradorestaurante.com; Tv das Pedras Negras 2; small plates €4.50-14; ☉ noon-3.30pm & 7-11pm Wed-Sat, noon-5pm Sun; 🛜)

Tasca Zé dos Cornos PORTUGUESE €€

13 ❌ MAP P80, A3

This family-owned Mouraria tavern welcomes regulars and first-timers with the same undivided attention. Space is tight so sharing tables is the norm and so is a line out the door. The menu contains typical Portuguese cuisine with an emphasis on pork (the ribs come highly recommended) and *bacalhau*

(dried salt-cod) grilled on the spot. Portions are generous. (☏ 218 869 641; www.facebook.com/ZeCornos; Beco Surradores 5; mains €5.50-12; ☉ 8am-11pm Mon-Sat)

Chapitô à Mesa PORTUGUESE €€

14 ❌ MAP P80, B4

At this circus school's casual cafe, the decidedly creative menu of Chef Bertílio Gomes is served alongside views worth writing home about. His modern takes include classic dishes (*bacalhau à Brás,* pork cheeks with clams, baked octopus with sweet potatoes and tomato frittata) that go swimmingly with a drop of Quinta da Silveira Reserva wine. (☏ 218 875 077; www.chapito.org; Rua Costa do Castelo 7; mains €19-21; ☉ noon-midnight Mon-Fri, 7.30-11pm Sat & Sun; 🛜)

Dine with Aunty 🍽️

It's nearly impossible to find a quality restaurant in Alfama that doesn't exist for tourism purposes, but there is one. Even Portuguese President Marcelo Rebelo de Sousa has been seduced by the homestyle food and crack-up character of **Ti-Natércia** (Map p80, E3; 📞218 862 133; Rua Escola Gerais 54; mains €5-12; ⏰7pm-midnight Tue-Fri, noon-3pm & 7pm-midnight Sat) – literally, 'Aunt Natércia' – a one-woman show deep in the heart of Alfama.

Santa Clara dos Cogumelos   INTERNATIONAL €€

15 ✕ MAP P80, F2

Mushroom fans unite! This Italian-owned, Italian-executed restaurant in the old Campo de Santa Clara market hall is simply magic. The menu devotes proper patronage to the humble *cogumelo* (mushroom). The organic shiitake *à bulhão pato* (with garlic and coriander) and the porcini ice cream with glazed chestnuts are outstanding. (📞218 870 661; www.santaclaradoscogumelos. com; Campo de Santa Clara 7; petiscos €4.50-11, mains €12-25; ⏰7.30-11pm Tue-Sun & 1-3pm Sat; 🛜🌱)

Cantinho do Aziz   MOZAMBICAN €€

16 ✕ MAP P80, A3

Hidden away in a narrow alleyway in the culturally diverse quarter of Mouraria, festive Cantinho do Aziz

gets top marks for excellent Mozambican cuisine. When you can't stomach any more sardine or *bacalhau,* head here for highly recommended *pulao do cabrito* (curried goat), *chacuti de cabrito* (goat in dark coconut sauce) or *makoufe* (shrimp and crab curry with peanut and coconut rice). (📞218 876 472; www.cantinhodoaziz. com; Rua de São Lourenço 3-5; mains €12-17; ⏰noon-11pm; 🛜🌱)

Princesa do Castelo   CAFE, VEGAN €€

17 ✕ MAP P80, C3

This chirpy, cash-only vegan cafe, run by a good-vibes Bangalorean, positively radiates good health with vegetarian, vegan, macrobiotic and sattvic dishes that play up the wild and the organic. Every day is different (there might be Mexican quinoa chilli with fried bananas, or tomato peanut rice with edamame aubergine curry), and the cafe offers Lisbon's only vegan *pastéis de nata*. (www.facebook.com/prince sadocastelorestaurantevegetariano; Rua do Salvador 64A; mains €10.50; ⏰noon-midnight Tue-Sun; 🛜🌱)

Santo António de Alfama   PORTUGUESE €€

18 ✕ MAP P80, D5

This bistro wins the award for Lisbon's loveliest summer courtyard: all vines, twittering budgerigars and fluttering laundry (though you'll struggle to find it at all in winter when the vines are bare). The interior is a silver-screen shrine, while the menu stars tasty *petiscos* (appetisers): breaded brie with raspberry compote, blood sausage with apple purée, as well as more-filling traditional Portuguese dishes. (📞218 881 328; www.siteantonio.com; Beco de São Miguel 7; mains €13.50-19.50; 🕐12.30pm-2am; 🛜)

Drinking

Memmo Alfama   BAR

19 🚇 MAP P80, C5

Wow, what a view! Alfama unfolds like origami from the stylishly decked roof terrace of the Memmo Alfama hotel. It's a perfect sun-downer place, with dreamy vistas over the rooftops, spires and down to the Rio Tejo. Cocktails cost €7.50 to €10. (www.memmoalfama. com; Tv das Merceeiras 27; 🕐noon-midnight; 🛜)

Lux-Frágil   CLUB

20 🚇 MAP P80, H2

Lisbon's ice-cool, must-see club, glammy Lux hosts big-name DJs spinning electro and house. It was started by late Lisbon nightlife impresario Marcel Reis and is part-owned by John Malkovich. Grab a spot on the terrace to see the sun rise over the Rio Tejo, or chill like a king or queen on the throne-like giant interior chairs. (www.luxfragil. com; Av Infante D Henrique, Armazém A, Cais de Pedra; 🕐11pm-6am Thu-Sat)

Copenhagen Coffee Lab   COFFEE

21 🚇 MAP P80, D3

The third location of this Danish-based speciality coffee house

Mesa de Frades (p89)

Fabulous Fado

There is no better way to tune into the Portuguese psyche, some say, than by listening to fado: plaintive, bittersweet music overflowing with emotional intensity. Ask locals what fado means and you'll get a different answer every time. And indeed, the more you listen to it, the more you realise how diverse the genre is. As one *fadista* (singer of fado) sagely put it: 'Fado is life itself: happiness, sadness, poetry, history.'

The Origins of Fado

Fado's origins are largely traceable to the backstreets of working-class Alfama. The ditties of homesick sailors, the poetic ballads of the Moors, the bluesy songs of Brazilian slaves – all are cited as possible influences, and no doubt fado is a blend of these and more. Central to all forms of fado is *saudade*, a hard-to-translate, distinctly Portuguese concept redolent of nostalgic longing. This often underpins recurring themes in fado such as destiny (*fado* means 'fate'), remorse, heartbreak and loneliness. In Lisbon, fado typically consists of a solo vocalist singing to the accompaniment of a 12-stringed Portuguese guitar and viola.

Famous Fadistas

If fado was born in Alfama, it was Amália Rodrigues (1920–99) who took it to the world with her heartbreaking trills and poetic soul. The so-called Rainha do Fado (Queen of Fado) still holds a special place in the hearts of the Portuguese. More recently, *fadistas* have continued to broaden fado's scope and appeal – often adding a pinch of blues, a splash of Argentine tango or a dash of flamenco. The best known of the new generation *fadistas* is Mariza, whose 2007 *Concerto em Lisboa* and 2008 *Terra* albums received Latin Grammy nominations.

Fado in Alfama

Wander through Alfama today and you'll almost certainly hear the strains of fado drifting from open windows of dimly-lit clubs. Performances range from light-hearted *fado vadio*, a kind of jam session where amateurs take turns to sing, to full professional acts. Which you prefer is a matter of taste. Wherever you go, when the lights go down, the audience falls silent – a sign of respect for the song of the soul.

is the perfect pit stop while wandering the cinematic lanes of Alfama. (www.copenhagencoffeelab. com; Rua das Escolas Gerais 34; ☺8am-7pm; 🕾)

Quiosque 8ª Colina   CRAFT BEER

22 🚇 MAP P80, D1

This Largo da Graça kiosk of nearby microbrewery 8ª Colina serves five taps of their sudsy wares – brewed just 170m away – in a pleasant public square setting. (www.oitavacolina.pt; Largo da Graça; ⏰noon-8pm Tue-Thu, to midnight Fri & Sat, 2-8pm Sun)

Portas do Sol   BAR

23 🚇 MAP P80, C4

Near one of Lisbon's iconic viewpoints, this sun-drenched terrace is a great place to sip cocktails (€7) while taking in magnificent river views. DJs bring animation to the darkly lit industrial interior on weekends. (www.portasdosol.pt; Largo das Portas do Sol; ⏰10am-1am Sun-Thu, to 2am Fri & Sat; 🛜)

Outro Lardo   CRAFT BEER

24 🚇 MAP P80, B6

The least beer-geeky of Lisbon's craft-beer bars, Sé's Outro Lardo offers eight artisanal brews on tap and 250 or so by the bottle, with an obvious emphasis on Portugal's rising scene. It's a good spot to get hopped up among various rooms of tattered leather sofas and mismatched tables. (www.facebook.com/OutroLadoLisboa; Beco do Arco Escuro 1; ⏰4pm-1am Tue-Thu, to 2am Fri & Sat; 🛜)

Entertainment

Senhor Fado   LIVE MUSIC

25 ⭐ MAP P80, F4

Small and lantern-lit, this is a cosy spot for fado vadio. Fadista Ana Marina and guitarist Duarte Santos make a great double act. (📞914 431 971; www.sr-fado.com; Rua dos Remédios 176; ⏰8pm-2am Wed-Sat)

Tasca Bela   LIVE MUSIC

26 ⭐ MAP P80, F3

This intimate spot features live fado on Wednesday, Friday, Saturday and Sunday, and eclectic cultural fare on other nights. Although there is a €19 minimum spend, unlike most fado houses you won't have to buy a pricey meal, as it's an appetisers-and-drinks kind of place. (📞926 077 511; www.facebook.com/bela.vinhosepetiscos; Rua dos Remédios 190; ⏰8.30pm-3am Tue-Sun)

A Baiuca   LIVE MUSIC

27 ⭐ MAP P80, D5

On a good night, going to A Baiuca is like gate-crashing a family party. It's a special place with fado vadio, where spectators hiss if anyone dares to chat during the singing. There's a €25 minimum spend, which is as tough to swallow as the food, though the fado is spectacular. (📞218 867 284; Rua de São Miguel 20; ⏰8pm-midnight Thu-Mon)

Mesa de Frades   LIVE MUSIC

28 ⭐ MAP P80, F4

A magical place to hear fado, tiny Mesa de Frades used to be a chapel. It's tiled with exquisite azulejos and has just a handful of tables. (📞917 029 436; www.facebook.com/mesadefradeslisboa; Rua dos Remédios 139A; prix-fixe show €50; ⏰8pm-2.30am Mon-Sat)

Damas   LIVE MUSIC

29 ⭐ MAP P80, D2

Restaurant, bar and alternative concert hall, Damas has given the cool kids a reason to climb the hill to Graça since its opening in 2015. There's always an eclectic mix of sound here and it's often free. (www.facebook.com/pg/DAMASLISBOA; Rua do Operário 60; ⏰1pm-2am Tue, 6pm-2am Wed & Thu, to 4am Fri & Sat)

Shopping

Cortiço & Netos   HOMEWARES

30 🔒 MAP P80, C2

A wall of fabulous *azulejos* greets you as you enter this special space. It's the vision of brothers Pedro, João, Ricardo and Tiago Cortiço, whose grandfather dedicated more than 30 years to gathering and selling discontinued Portuguese industrial tiles.

Reviving the family trade, the brothers are experts on the *azulejo*

and how it can be interpreted today. (www.corticoenetos.com; Calçada de Santo André 66; ⏰10am-1pm & 2-7pm Mon-Sat)

A Arte da Terra   GIFTS & SOUVENIRS

31 🔒 MAP P80, C5

In the stables of a centuries-old bishop's palace, A Arte da Terra brims with authentic Portuguese crafts including Castello Branco embroideries, nativity figurines, hand-painted *azulejos,* fado CDs and quality cork goods.

Some goods are beautifully lit in former troughs. (www.aartedaterra.pt; Rua de Augusto Rosa 40; ⏰11am-8pm)

Feira da Ladra

O Voo da Andorinha

GIFTS & SOUVENIRS

32 🔒 MAP P80, C5

Candy-bright beads, embroidered accessories and quirky furnishings – you'll find all of this and more at this adorable boutique representing some 50 Lisbon-area artists near the cathedral. (www.facebook. com/ovoodaandorinha; Rua do Barão 22; ⏲11am-7.30pm Mon-Sat)

Era Uma Vez Um Sonho

TOYS

33 🔒 MAP P80, C5

For over 20 years this enchanting shop has dealt in unique puppets, stuffed animals, puzzles and illustrated books, all handcrafted in Portugal. (www.eraumavezumsonho. pt; Rua do Barão 22; ⏲10am-8pm Mon-Sat)

Só.Sé

DESIGN

34 🔒 MAP P80, C5

To meet Portuguese designer Jorge Moita and see his La.Ga bags – his 'UFOs' – visit his gallery, design studio and freeform creative space in Alfama. The striking handbags, made of super-lightweight, incredibly resistant Tyvek, bear the creatively unique hallmarks of female prisoners, designers and artists. (📞937 103 093; www.facebook.com/ krvkurva; Beco do Quebras Costas 4; ⏲7am-10pm Tue-Sat, 7am-2pm Sun)

Feira da Ladra

MARKET

35 🔒 MAP P80, F2

Browse and haggle for buried treasures at this massive flea market. You'll find old records, coins, baggy pants, dog-eared poetry books and other attic junk. (www.cm-lisboa.pt; Campo de Santa Clara; ⏲9am-5pm Tue & Sat)

Alfama, Castelo & Graça Shopping

Worth a Trip 🔭

Take in Stunning Tiles at the Museu Nacional do Azulejo

When Queen Dona Leonor founded the Convento do Madre de Deus in 1509, she surely had no idea that the convent would become a tribute to the azulejo (hand-painted tile). This exceptional museum unravels 500 years of Portuguese history and craftwork. A day here takes you through chapels with religious panels, corridors of hunting scenes and rooms dancing with geometric detail.

☎ 218 100 340
www.museudoazulejo.pt
Rua Madre de Deus 4
adult/child €5/free
🕙 10am-6pm Tue-Sun

Sala de Grande Vista de Lisboa

Tucked away on the 2nd floor, the early-18th-century Great View of Lisbon is the museum's undisputed highlight. Attributed to Spanish tile painter Gabriel del Barco, the huge panoramic panel beautifully encapsulates the city before the earthquake struck in 1755. Pick out Lisbon's seven hills, riverfront and landmarks past and present in the intricately painted blue-and-white *azulejos*.

Nossa Senhora da Vida

Made up of 1498 tiles, the late-16th-century Altarpiece of Our Lady of Life is one of Portugal's earliest *azulejo* masterpieces. Trompe l'œil diamond-tip tiles fringe the base, while ivy-clad columns frame erudite evangelists St John and St Luke, and the centrepiece scene showing the Adoration of the Shepherds.

Church

This Mannerist church in high baroque style is a breathtakingly lavish gilt, fresco and *azulejo* confection. Cherubs appear to flutter above the gilded altarpieces, and the ceiling is festooned with frescoes depicting the life of the Virgin and Christ. Look for late-17th-century Dutch tile panels showing Moses and the Burning Bush, Franciscans at prayer and the Cortege of Shepherds.

Capela de Santo António

On the 1st floor, this chapel is a shrine to Franciscan preacher St Anthony of Lisbon. Commissioned by King João V, it's a stellar example of Portuguese baroque, with parquetry flooring, intricate wood carvings and a prized 18th-century terracotta crib. The blue-and-white *azulejo* panels show scenes from the life of hermit saints and the miracles of St Anthony.

★ Top Tips

o The permanent collection is huge – allow two to three hours to do the museum justice.

o Free English audio guides are available (and also for Android mobile phones).

o Admission is free on Sunday until 2pm for Portuguese citizens/residents only.

o Money-saving combo tickets are available with Panteão Nacional (€7), plus Museu Nacional de Arte Antiga (€15), among others.

✗ Take a Break

Lodged in the former refectory, the **museum cafe** (snacks and mains are €5 to €9) is covered in 19th-century culinary *azulejos*. It opens onto a leafy courtyard and is an atmospheric place for a coffee and crêpe or a lunch special.

Explore ⊗
Belém

Atlantic breezes, grandiose nautical monuments and boats gliding along the wide Rio Tejo cast you back to those pioneering days of the Age of Discoveries, when the world was Portugal's colonial oyster. And at dusk, when the crowds subside and the softening light paints the monastery's Manueline turrets gold, this riverside neighbourhood is yours alone for exploring.

The Short List

○ **Mosteiro dos Jerónimos (p96)** *Gaze upon the stunning Manueline cloisters inside this monastery.*

○ **Antiga Confeitaria de Belém (p105)** *Wallow in the sweet satisfaction of a piping-hot, custard-cream-filled pastel de Belém.*

○ **Museu Coleção Berardo (p98)** *Get your fix amid a world-class collection of abstract, surrealist and pop art.*

○ **Feitoria (p108)** *Settle in for a trip-defining, Michelin-starred dining adventure at chef João Rodrigues' contemporary waterfront temple.*

Getting There & Around

🚋 Easy, quick and scenic. Tram 15E runs from Praça da Figueira to Belém via Alcântara (around 30 minutes' journey). Tram 18 runs from Cais do Sodré to Ajuda.

🚌 Bus 28 operates frequently between Belém and central Lisbon, stopping in Praça do Comércio and Cais do Sodré.

🚆 The suburban Comboios de Portugal Cais do Sodré–Cascais train line runs from central Lisbon in eight minutes.

Neighbourhood Map on p102

Top Experience 📷

Witness the Masterpiece of Mosteiro dos Jerónimos

Diogo de Boitaca's creative vision and King Manuel I's gold-laden coffers gave rise to this fantasy fairy tale of a monastery, founded in 1501 to trumpet Vasco da Gama's discovery of a sea route to India. Now a Unesco World Heritage Site, Jerónimos was once populated by monks whose spiritual job for four centuries was to comfort sailors and pray for the king's soul.

◎ MAP P102, C2

www.mosteirojeronimos.pt

Praça do Império

adult/child €10/5, free Sun until 2pm for Portuguese citizens/residents only

🕙10am-6.30pm Tue-Sun Jun-Sep, to 5.30pm Oct-May

Igreja Santa Maria de Belém

Entering the church through the western portal, you'll notice tree-trunk-like columns growing into the ceiling, itself a spiderweb of stone. Navigator Vasco da Gama is interred in the lower chancel, left of the entrance, opposite 16th-century poet Luís Vaz de Camões. From the upper choir is a superb view of the church.

Cloister

The honey-stone Manueline cloister drips with organic detail in its delicately scalloped arches, twisting auger-shell turrets and columns intertwined with leaves, vines and knots. Pick out symbols of the age, like the armillary sphere and the cross of the Military Order, plus gargoyles and fantastical beasties on the upper level. In the north wing of the cloister, you'll find the tomb of Portugal's most famous and important literary figure, the great Fernando Pessoa, whose remains were transferred here to a tomb by master sculptor Lagoa Henriques in 1985.

Chapter House & Refectory

Vines, flowers, cherubs and reliefs of St Jerome and St Bernard frame the Chapter House's 16th-century portal holding the tomb of Portuguese historian Alexandre Herculano. In the vaulted refectory, 18th-century *azulejo* (hand-painted tile) panels depict the miracle of the loaves and fishes, and scenes from the life of Joseph. António Campelo's evocative mural shows the Adoration of the Shepherds.

South Portal

A riot of pinnacles and lacy stonework, the South Portal is the elaborate handiwork of 16th-century architect João de Castilho. The figure of Nossa Senhora de Belém (Our Lady of Bethlehem) sits surrounded by apostles, prophets and angels. Note Henry the Navigator, high on a pedestal, and the tympanum above the door, revealing scenes from the life of St Jerome.

★ Top Tips

o Try to visit in the morning on clear days, when bright sunlight illuminates the church's stained-glass windows in a kaleidoscopic show.

o Save a few euros by buying a combined ticket with the Museu Nacional de Arqueologia for €12, or enter free with the Lisboa Card.

o Arrive early or late to appreciate the monastery at its serene best.

✗ Take a Break

Grab a *pastel de Belém* (custard tart) at nearby Antiga Confeitaria de Belém (p105) and enjoy it among the leafy environs of a garden across the street from the monastery.

One of Lisbon's iconic vintage trams has been born again as the nicely chilled **Banana Cafe** (www.facebook.com/ bananacafe.lisboa), with tables set up under the trees. It's a relaxed spot for a coffee, sangria or light snack.

Top Experience 📷

Catch Must-See Modern Art at Museu Coleção Berardo

With works by Picasso, Warhol, Yves Klein, Pollock, Miró and Lichtenstein, this gallery holds its own with the Tates and Guggenheims of the world. Yet, incredibly, it's still under the must-see sightseeing radar. Dadaism, minimalism, kinetic art, surrealism and conceptualism – the mind-blowing collection spans the spectrum of modern and contemporary art. Go. Go today.

◉ MAP P102, C3

www.museuberardo.pt

Centro Cultural de Belém, Praça do Império

adult/student/child under 6yr €5/2.50/free, free Sat

🕓 10am-7pm

British & American Pop Art

Race back to the 1950s and '60s contemplating pop-art masterpieces from both sides of the pond. Warhol's silk-screened portrait of Judy Garland, *Ten Foot Flowers*, *Brillo Box* tower and *Campbell's Soup* steal the limelight. Look too for David Hockney's *Picture Emphasising Stillness* and Lichtenstein's *Interior with Restful Painting*.

Cubism & Dadaism

Several abstract pieces by Picasso, daddy of cubism, are on display, among them his early-20th-century *Tête de Femme* and *Femme dans un Fauteuil*. The anti-war Dadaists also sought to break with conventional art forms. Emblematic of the movement is French artist Marcel Duchamp's 1914 *Le Porte Bouteilles (Bottle Dryer)*.

Surrealism

Explore outlandish works by Man Ray, such as his mixed-media *Café Man Ray* and *Talking Picture*, and other standouts of the movement such as Magritte's spacey *Le Gouffre Argenté*, Joan Miró's *Figure à la Bougie*, Max Ernst's inky *Paysage Noir* and Jean Arp's teardrop-like *Feuilles Placées Selon les Lois du Hasard*. For a different perspective, zoom in on the monochromatic photography of Lisbon-born Fernando Lemos.

Modern & Contemporary Sculpture

Sculptures stopping you in your tracks by the entrance include Niki de Saint-Phalle's curvaceous, rainbow-bright *Les Baigneuses (Swimmers)*, Pedro Cabrita Reis' industrial-meets-abstract *Amarração*, and Joana Vasconcelos' green wine-bottle wonder, *Nectar*. Inside, look for bronze creations by Antony Gormley, Barry Flanagan and Henry Moore.

★ Top Tips

○ Admission is free all day Saturday.

○ Pick up a free guide at the entrance for some background on the permanent exhibition.

○ Visit the website for details of upcoming temporary exhibitions; these are held on level 0.

○ Allow at least a couple of hours to do this gallery justice.

✕ Take a Break

Centro Cultural de Belém is also home to hip TOPO Belém (p108) – grab food or a cocktail with a view!

Hidden down a small alley a short walk away, cosy Enoteca de Belém (p107) is a wonderful, wine-centric spot for modernised Portuguese fare.

Belém Catch Must-See Modern Art at Museu Coleção Berardo

Walking Tour 🥾

Belém's Age of Discoveries

A stroll through nautical-flavoured Belém, with its broad river views and exuberant Manueline architecture, catapults you back to Portugal's golden Age of Discoveries – the 15th and 16th centuries, when explorers like Vasco da Gama and Henry the Navigator set sail for lands rich in gold and spices aboard mighty caravels, and Portugal was but a drop in King Manuel I's colonial ocean.

Walk Facts

Start Praça do Império;
🚋 15E, 🚌 28

End Torre de Belém;
🚋 15E, 🚌 28

Length 2.5km; 1½ hours

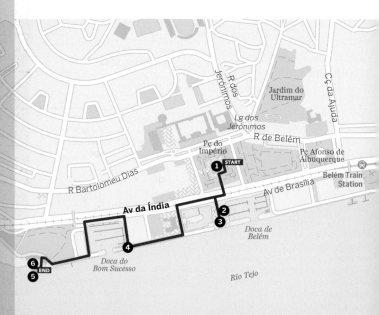

❶ Praça do Império

Even blasé locals never tire of the uplifting view of the **Mosteiro dos Jerónimos** (p96), **Museu Coleção Berardo** (p98) and Rio Tejo from this stately plaza, set around a fountain and fringed by box hedges. Note Age of Discoveries symbols, such as anchors and the cross of the Military Order, featured in flowers and foliage.

Fuel yourself for the walk by stopping for some of Lisbon's best Roman-style gelato at **Gelato Davvero** (p107) inside the **Centro Cultural de Belém** (p109).

❷ Maritime Map

Head across to the breezy riverfront promenade, looking down as you approach the Padrão dos Descobrimentos, to spot a **mosaic map** charting the routes of Portuguese mariners and the dates of colonisation, from the Azores (1427) to Calcutta (1498) and beyond.

❸ Padrão dos Descobrimentos

Like a caravel caught in mid-swell, the 56m-high **Padrão dos Descobrimentos** (p105) depicts Henry the Navigator and some of the major figures of Portuguese exploration. At the prow is Henry, while behind him are explorers Vasco da Gama, Diogo Cão, Fernão de Magalhães (Ferdinand Magellan) and 29 other greats. Take the lift (or puff up 267 steps) to the wind-swept miradouro for 360-degree views over the river.

❹ Doca do Bom Sucesso

Take a brisk walk along the riverfront to the Doca do Bom Sucesso, where you can watch the boats and seagulls while sipping drinks on the laid-back terrace of **Bar 38° 41'** (p108). Belém's waterfront is prime people-watching real estate for locals and tourists alike. Alternatively, this is a relaxed spot to dip into Luís Vaz de Camões' *The Lusiads*, an epic poem recounting Vasco da Gama's explorations.

❺ Torre de Belém

Feel the pull of the past and the breezes of the Atlantic as you gaze up at the **Torre de Belém** (p103), an early-16th-century icon of the Age of Discoveries and a prime example of whimsical Manueline style with its ribbed cupolas.

❻ Hidden Rhino

It's easy to miss one of Torre de Belém's most intriguing features. Below the western tower is a rhinoceros, a **stone carving** of the Indian rhino Manuel I shipped to Pope Leo X as a token of his esteem in 1515. The rhino never reached Rome – it drowned when the ship capsized – but Albrecht Dürer immortalised it in his famous woodcut.

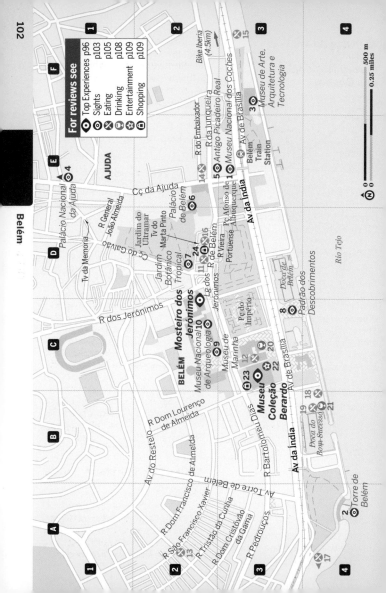

For reviews see

- 🔵 Top Experiences p96
- 🔶 Sights p103
- ✖️ Eating p105
- 🍷 Drinking p108
- 🎭 Entertainment p109
- 🛍️ Shopping p109

AJUDA

Palácio Nacional da Ajuda ▲🔵 4

Tv da Memória

R General João Almeida

Cç do Galvão

Jardim do Ultramar

Tv do Palácio de Belém

Jardim Botânico Tropical

Cç da Ajuda

🔵 6

Pç Afonso de Albuquerque

R de Belém 🔶 16

R Vieira Portuense

24

11

7

🔵 Mosteiro dos Jerónimos 10 🔵

Lg dos Jerónimos

R dos Jerónimos

BELÉM

Museu Nacional de Arqueologia 🔵 9

Museu de Marinha 🔵

12

23

Museu Coleção Berardo 🔵

22

20

R Dom Lourenço de Almeida

Pç do Império

Padrão dos Descobrimentos 8 🔵

Av de Brasília

Doca de Belém

Rio Tejo

Av da India

R Embaixador

R da Junqueira

Antigo Picadeiro Real 5 🔶

Museu Nacional dos Coches 🔵 1

Bike Iberia (4.5km)

Belém Train Station

Av de Brasília

🔵 3

Museu de Arte, Arquitetura e Tecnologia

✖️ 15

✖️ 14

Av do Restelo

R Bartolomeu Dias

R Dom Francisco de Almeida

R São Francisco Xavier ✖️ 13

R Tristão da Cunha

R Dom Cristóvão da Gama

R Pedrouços

Av da Torre de Belém

Av da India

Doca do Bom Sucesso

19 ✖️ 18

21

17 ✖️

2 🔵 Torre de Belém

N

0 500 m
0 0.25 miles

Sights

Museu Nacional dos Coches   MUSEUM

1 ⊙ MAP P102, E3

Cinderella wannabes delight in Portugal's most visited museum, which dazzles with its world-class collection of 70 17th- to 19th-century coaches in an ultramodern space that debuted in 2015. Don't miss Pope Clement XI's stunning ride, the scarlet-and-gold *Coach of the Oceans*, or the old royal riding school, Antigo Picadeiro Real, across the street. (www.museudoscoches.pt; Av da Índia 136; admission €8; ⊙10am-6pm Tue-Sun)

Torre de Belém   TOWER

2 ⊙ MAP P102, A4

Jutting out onto the Rio Tejo, this Unesco World Heritage–listed fortress epitomises the Age of Discoveries. You'll need to breathe in to climb the narrow spiral staircase to the tower, which affords sublime views over Belém and the river. (www.torrebelem.pt; Av de Brasília; adult/child €6/3, free Sun until 2pm for Portuguese citizens/residents only; ⊙10am-6.30pm Tue-Sun May Sep, to 5.30pm Oct-Apr)

Museu de Arte, Arquitetura e Tecnologia   MUSEUM

3 ⊙ MAP P102, F3

Lisbon's latest riverfront star is this low-rise, glazed-tiled structure that intriguingly hips and sways into ground-level exhibition halls. Visitors can walk over and under its reflective surfaces, which play with water, light and shadow, and pay homage to the city's intimate relationship with the sea. (MAAT; Art, Architecture & Technology Museum; www.maat.pt; Av de Brasília, Central Tejo; admission with/without Central Tejo €9/5; ⊙11am-7pm Wed-Mon)

Palácio Nacional da Ajuda   PALACE

4 ⊙ MAP P102, E1

Built in the early 19th century, this staggering neoclassical palace served as the royal residence from the 1860s until the end of the monarchy (1910). You can tour private apartments and state rooms, getting an eyeful of gilded furnishings and exquisite artworks dating back five centuries, as well as the queen's chapel, home to Portugal's only El Greco painting. It's a long uphill walk from Belém, or you can take tram 18E or several buses from downtown, including 760 from Praça do Comércio. (☎213 637 095; www.palacioajuda.gov.pt; Largo da Ajuda; adult/child €5/free, free Sun until 2pm for Portuguese citizens/residents only; ⊙10am-6pm Thu-Tue)

Antigo Picadeiro Real   MUSEUM

5 ⊙ MAP P102, E2

Lisbon's original coach museum is now home to just seven of these majestic 18th-century four-wheeled works of art, but it's worth also visiting the stuccoed, frescoed halls of the former royal riding stables built by Italian architect Giacomo Azzolini in 1726 – a far more fitting and palatial rest home than the modern monolith, Museu Nacional dos Coches (p103), across the street. (Old Royal Riding School; www.museudoscoches.pt; Praça Afonso de Albuquerque; admission €4, with Museu Nacional dos Coches €10, free Sun to 2pm for Portuguese citizens/residents only; ⊙10am-6pm Tue-Sun)

Palácio de Belém
HISTORIC BUILDING

6 ◎ MAP P102, E2

The salmon-slabbed 16th-century Belém Palace is Portugal's official presidential residence and office (though the country's previous president, Cavaco Silva, chose to live in his own home). Tours in Portuguese, English and French are available on Saturday only, with just 150 spots up for grabs (book in advance via email). Alternatively, the small but fascinating **Museu da Presidência da República** (Museum of the Presidency of the Republic; Map p102, D2; www.museu.presidencia.pt; adult/child €2.50/free, with Palácio de Belém €5; ⊙10am-6pm Tue-Sun) is open most of the week. (Belém Palace; 🕿213 614 660; www.presidencia.pt; Praça Afonso de Albuquerque; adult/child €5/free; ⊙10.30am-4.30pm Sat)

Jardim Botânico Tropical
GARDENS

7 ◎ MAP P102, D2

Far from the madding crowd, these botanical gardens bristle with hundreds of species, from date palms

Torre de Belém (p103)

to monkey-puzzle trees. Spread across 7 hectares, it's a peaceful, shady retreat on a sweltering summer's day. A highlight is the Macau garden, complete with mini pagoda, where bamboo rustles and a cool stream trickles. (www.iict.pt/jbt; Largo dos Jerónimos; adult/child €2/1; ⏾10am-8pm May-Aug, shorter hours in winter)

Padrão dos Descobrimentos
MUSEUM

8 ◉ MAP P102, C3

The monolithic Padrão dos Descobrimentos, looking like a caravel frozen in midswell, was inaugurated in 1960 on the 500th anniversary of Henry the Navigator's death. The 56m-high limestone giant is chockfull of depictions of Age of Discoveries bigwigs. (Discoveries Monument; www.padraodosdescobrimentos.pt; Av de Brasília; adult/child €5/2.50; ⏾10am-7pm Mar-Sep, to 6pm Oct-Feb)

Museu de Marinha
MUSEUM

9 ◉ MAP P102, C2

The Museu de Marinha is a nautical flashback to the Age of Discoveries, with its armadas of model ships, cannonballs and shipwreck booty. Dig for buried treasure such as Vasco da Gama's portable wooden altar, 17th-century globes (note Australia's absence) and the polished private quarters of UK-built royal yacht *Amélia*. A separate building houses royal barges, 19th-century firefighting machines and seaplanes. (Naval Museum; http://ccm.marinha.pt/pt/museu; Praça do Império; adult/child €6.50/3.25, free 1st Sun of month; ⏾10am-6pm Tue-Sun May-Sep, to 5pm Oct-Apr)

Museu Nacional de Arqueologia
MUSEUM

10 ◉ MAP P102, C2

Housed in the western wing of Mosteiro dos Jerónimos (p96), the intriguing stash here contains mesolithic flint stones, Egyptian mummies inside elaborately painted sarcophagi, and beautifully wrought Bronze Age jewellery. Even more curious is the collection of statues dedicated to Roman deities. (National Archaeology Museum; www.museuarqueologia.pt; Praça do Império; adult/child €5/free, free Sun to 2pm for Portuguese citizens/residents only; ⏾10am-6pm Tue-Sun)

Eating

Antiga Confeitaria de Belém
PASTRIES €

11 ✗ MAP P102, D2

Since 1837 this patisserie has been transporting locals to sugar-coated nirvana with heavenly *pastéis de Belém*. The crisp pastry nests are filled with custard cream, baked at 200°C for that perfect golden crust, then lightly dusted with cinnamon. Admire *azulejos* in the vaulted rooms or devour a still-warm tart at the counter and try to guess the secret ingredient. (Pastéis de Belém; www.pasteisdebelem.pt; Rua de Belém 84-92; pastries from €1.10; ⏾8am-11pm Oct-Jun, to midnight Jul-Sep)

The Age of Discoveries

The 15th and 16th centuries were Portugal's golden age, when the small kingdom built itself into a massive imperial power and Europe's wealthiest monarchy. Dom João set the ball rolling when he conquered Ceuta, Morocco, in 1415. It was a turning point in Portuguese history.

Manueline Riches

Portugal's biggest breakthrough came in 1497 during the reign of Manuel I, when Vasco da Gama reached southern India. With African gold and slaves, and spices from the East, Portugal was soon rolling in riches. Manuel I was so thrilled by the discoveries that he ordered a frenzied building spree in celebration of the age. Top of his list was the Mosteiro dos Jerónimos in Belém, later to become his pantheon.

Enter Spain

Spain had also jumped on the exploration bandwagon and was soon disputing Portuguese claims. Christopher Columbus' 1492 'discovery' of America led to a fresh outburst of jealous conflict. It was resolved by the pope in the 1494 Treaty of Tordesillas, which divided the world between the two powers along a line 370 leagues west of Cape Verde.

Epic Voyage

The rivalry spurred the first circumnavigation of the world. In 1519 Portuguese navigator Fernão de Magalhães (Ferdinand Magellan), his allegiance transferred to Spain after a tiff with Manuel I, set off to prove the Spice Islands (Moluccas) lay in Spanish 'territory'. He perished in the Philippines in 1521 but one of his ships reached the islands and then sailed home via the Cape of Good Hope, proving the earth was round.

Sinking Ship

By the 1570s, the huge cost of expeditions and an empire was taking its toll. Sebastião's mortal defeat at the 1578 Battle of Alcácer-Quibir launched a downward spiral. When his successor, Cardinal Henrique, died in 1580, Felipe II of Spain fought for and won the throne. This marked the end of centuries of independence and Portugal's glorious moment on the world stage.

Gelato Davvero

GELATO €

12 MAP P102, C3

It's now worth ducking into Centro Cultural de Belém for something other than performances and contemporary art: 22 flavours of excellent gelato lie in wait at Gelato Davvero's latest location. Filippo Licitra's creations often push the envelope – avocado, salmon, curried mango – but all the classics are here as well. (www.facebook.com/gelatodavvero; Praça do Império, Centro Cultural de Belém; small/medium/large €2/3/4; ☺noon-8pm Sun & Mon, to 9pm Tue-Thu, to 11pm Fri & Sat)

Pastelaria Restelo   BAKERY €

13 🍴 MAP P102, A2

Better known as Pastelaria O Careca ('The Bald Guy') among locals, this simple *pastelaria* (pastry and cake shop) flanking a small plaza has been dishing out Lisbon's sweetest croissants since 1954. It's definitely worth heading a few blocks inland from the waterfront for the doughy, sugar-coated goodness. (www.pastelariaocareca.pt; Rua Duarte Pacheco Pereira 11D; croissants €1.20; ☺8am-8pm Mon & Wed-Sat, 8.30am-8pm Sun)

Alecrim & Manjerona   CAFE €

14 🍴 MAP P102, E2

Tucked away from the [   ] side street, Alecrim & [   ] s a cute grocery store, [   ] wine bar rolled into o[   ] delicious homemad[   ] tarts, it rustles up w[   ] specials. (www.faceb[   ] alecrimmanjeroname[   ] Embaixador 143; ligh[   ]es €2.75-8; ☺10am-6p[   ]

SUD Lisboa Te[   ]   AN €€

15 🍴 MAP P102, F3

This hot riverside s[   ] es nicely with an afternoon visiting the

MAAT next door. Upscale Italian is served with occasional Portuguese and Asian flourishes (baked grouper with lemon capers sauce and pak choi cake; cocoa-bean-crusted New Zealand rack of lamb) alongside a design-forward space highlighted by a coconut-strewn bamboo ceiling. Cocktails (€9 to €14) sure go down nicely on the plush patio. (📞211 592 702; www.sudlisboa.com; Av de Brasília, Pavilhão Poente; mains €14-32, pizzas €14-19; ☺11am-2am; 🛜)

Enoteca de Belém   PORTUGUESE €€

16 🍴 MAP P102, D2

Tucked down a quiet lane just off Belém's main thoroughfare, this casual wine bar serves modernised Portuguese classics (fantastic octopus, Iberian pork), matched by an excellent selection of full-bodied Douro reds and refreshing Alentejan whites. The experience – led by well-trained servers particularly adept at gravitating you towards a juice that marries with your tastes – is distinctively memorable. (📞213 631 511; www.travessadaermida.com; Tv do Marta Pinto 10; mains €17-20; ☺1-11pm; 🛜)

Darwin's Café   CAFE €€

17 🍴 MAP P102, A4

This trendy evolution-themed cafe suffers from a bit of scholarly overreach inside (though the big, round banquettes are great for groups), but its elevated terrace affords postcard-perfect views of the Rio Tejo and Torre de Belém. It

Pastéis de Belém 🍽

The origins of heavenly *pastéis de Belém* (aka *pastéis de nata*) stretch back to an early-19th-century sugarcane refinery next to the Mosteiro dos Jerónimos. The liberal revolution swept through Portugal in 1820 and by 1834 all monasteries had been shut down, the monks expelled. Desperate to survive, some clerics saw the light in all that sugar, and *pastéis de Belém* were born. The top-secret custard tart recipe hasn't changed since then and shall forever serve as a reminder that calories need not be sinful. Amen.

draws a fashion-forward local crowd with sophisticated pastas, risottos and the like, as well as an extensive list of bubbly by the flute. (📞210 480 222; www.darwincafe.com; Av de Brasília, Ala B; mains €16.50-26.50; 🕑12.30-4pm Mon, 12.30-3.30pm, 4.30-6.30pm & 7.30-11pm Tue-Sun)

A Margem   FUSION €€

18 ✖ MAP P102, B4

Well positioned near the river's edge, this small, sun-drenched cube of glass and white stone boasts an open patio and large windows facing the Tejo and dramatic sunsets over the Torre de Belém. Service isn't thrilling, but locals come for fresh salads, cheese plates, bruschetta and other light bites that go nicely with wine and various drinks. Sunglasses are essential. (📞914 736 191; www.amargem.com; Doca do Bom Sucesso; salads €10-14, wines €3.50-5; 🕑10am-1am Apr-Oct, to 7.30pm Nov-Mar)

Feitoria   MODERN PORTUGUESE €€€

19 ✖ MAP P102, B4

A defining dining experience awaits at chef João Rodrigues' slick, contemporary, Michelin-starred restaurant overlooking the riverfront. Rich textures and clean, bright flavours dominate throughout three tasting menus, which showcase Portugal's rich and vibrant bounty. (📞210 400 208; www.restaurantefeitoria.com; Altis Belém Hotel, Doca do Bom Sucesso; mains €85-135, tasting menus €75-120, with wine €130-195; 🕑7.30-10pm Mon-Sat; 🛜)

Drinking

TOPO Belém   BAR

20 🍷 MAP P102, C3

Revive museum-weary eyes at hard-to-find Topo, on the 3rd floor of the Centro Cultural de Belém. The space and river-facing terrace provide an attractive spot for sipping cocktails (€9 to €10), and there's upscale Portuguese cuisine. (www.topo-lisboa.pt; Praça do Império, Centro Cultural de Belém; 🕑noon-midnight Sun-Thu, to 2am Fri & Sat; 🛜)

Bar 38° 41'   BAR

21 🍷 MAP P102, B4

Watch boats bob on the water over coffee or cocktails (€8 to €10)

BRASIL NUT/GETTY IMAGES ©

Antiga Confeitaria de Belém (p105)

at this stylish, dressed-in-black dockside lounge bar. Guest DJs liven things up Thursday through Sunday in summer. (☎ 210 400 210; www.altishotels.com; Altis Belém Hotel, Doca do Bom Sucesso; ⏰11am-1am)

Entertainment

Centro Cultural de Belém   THEATRE

22 ⭐ MAP P102, C3

The CCB presents a diverse program spanning experimental jazz, contemporary ballet, boundary-crossing plays and performances by the Portuguese Chamber Orchestra. Buy tickets at the box office (open 11am to 8pm). (CCB; ☎ 213 612 400; www.ccb.pt; ⏰8am-8pm Mon-Fri, 10am-6pm Sat & Sun)

Shopping

Hangar Design Store   DESIGN

23 🔒 MAP P102, C3

This shop's owner has assembled a well-curated collection of top design-forward objects from Portugal and beyond. (www.hangar.pt; Rua Bartolomeu Dias, Loja 1, Centro Cultural de Belém; ⏰11am-7.30pm)

Original Lisboa   ARTS & CRAFTS

24 🔒 MAP P102, D2

As its name suggests, this is the place to find original gifts by young Portuguese designers. Playful jewellery, bags emblazoned with Lisbon trams, cork creations, *azulejo* coasters, paintings and fashion – it's all at this one-stop shop. (Rua de Belém 82; ⏰11am-7.30pm Tue-Sun)

Explore ✦

Parque das Nações

A shining model of urban regeneration, Parque das Nações has almost single-handedly propelled the city into the 21st century since Expo '98. Glittering high-rises, sci-fi concert halls, and Europe's longest bridge and second-largest aquarium rise above a river so wide it could be the sea. This is the Lisbon of the future.

○ **Oceanário de Lisboa (p112)** Diving into the underwater world of Europe's largest indoor aquarium, a conservation-conscious oceanarium that captivates all ages.

○ **Ponte Vasco da Gama (p116)** Ogling Europe's longest bridge at sunset, a no-filter-necessary cable-stayed stunner across the Rio Tejo.

○ **Casa Bota Feijão (p116)** Dunking juicy, spit-roasted suckling pig into peppery garlic sauce at this simple local favourite.

○ **Gare do Oriente (p115)** Pondering the best photo angles at Santiago Calatrava's Gothic-influenced, space-age train station.

Getting There & Around

M The red line speeds you between central Lisbon and Oriente in around 20 minutes; services run frequently.

🚌 Services connecting Parque das Nações to central Lisbon include the 708 to Martim Moniz (via the airport, which is just three metro stops from Oriente).

Neighbourhood Map on p114

Ponte Vasco da Gama (p116) OLEDJIO/SHUTTERSTOCK ©

Top Experience 📷

Dive into the Mammoth Oceanário Aquarium

Europe's second-largest aquarium has an eye-popping 8000 marine creatures splashing in 7 million litres of water. Sand tiger sharks, stingrays, pufferfish and sunfish swim in the mammoth central tank, while puffins, penguins and sea otters are featured in North Atlantic, Antarctic, Pacific and Indian Ocean exhibitions. Conservation is the name of the game, with no circus hoopla.

◉ MAP P114, C4

www.oceanario.pt

Doca dos Olivais

adult/child €15/10, including temporary exhibition €18/12

🕙 10am-8pm, to 7pm in winter

Pacific Sea Otters

Make for the Pacific to coo over the Oceanário's superstar sea otters: Maré and Micas. The duo are ridiculously cute as they turn somersaults, swim placidly on their backs and groom their fur.

Central Tank

Standing in front of this whopper of a tank, or 'global ocean', is like scuba diving without getting wet. Speckled zebra sharks, globular sunfish, shoals of neon fish and manta rays – the flying carpets of the underwater world – hold audiences captive.

Sleeping with the Sharks

Who needs bedtime stories when you can scare your kids (and maybe yourself) silly by sleeping next to a shark tank? Costing €60 per person, these midnight *Jaws* encounters zoom in on conservation and give you the run of the almost-empty Oceanário the next morning.

Penguins on Ice

Watch Magellanic and crested rockhopper penguins waddle and slide across the ice in the Antarctic exhibition, then go down to the subaquatic level to glimpse them swimming gracefully underwater.

Underwater Close-Ups

Ghost-like moon jellyfish, giant octopuses, lacy sea dragons and big-belly sea horses are among the more unusual species splashing around in the tanks on the subaquatic level. Geeky fact for Nemo fans: clownfish are transsexual, with the dominant male eventually morphing into a female.

★ **Top Tips**

o Buy tickets online to jump the queue.

o Join a backstage tour for insights into what goes on behind the scenes.

o Don't use the flash on your camera – it frightens the fish.

o Pick up an audio guide for a running commentary of the exhibition.

o Plan your visit around feeding times: sea otters 10am, 12.45pm and 3.15pm; penguins 10am and 3pm; manta rays and sunfish 1pm; sharks 10.30am Monday and Friday; stingrays 11.15am Monday, Wednesday and Friday.

✗ **Take a Break**

The pizzeria Zero-Zero (p116), one of Lisbon's best, sits just across the street from the aquarium.

For impressive Rio Tejo and Ponte Vasco da Gama views, imbibe in a cocktail at River Lounge (p117) at the other end of Parque das Nações.

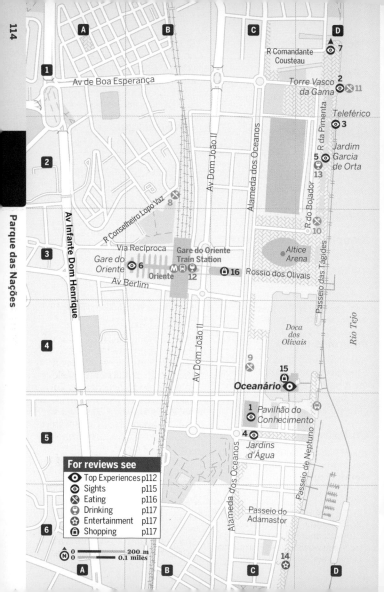

Parque das Nações

A1

B

C

D7

R Comandante Cousteau

Av de Boa Esperança

Torre Vasco da Gama 2 ✕11

Teleférico
3

R da Pimenta

5
13

Jardim Garcia de Orta

Av Dom João II

R Conselheiro Lopo Vaz

8

R do Bojador

10

R Via Recíproca

Gare do Oriente

Gare do Oriente Train Station

12

16

Rossio dos Olivais

Altice Arena

Av Berlim

Oriente

Av Infante Dom Henrique

Passeio das Tágides

Rio Tejo

Doca dos Olivais

9

15

Oceanário

Av Dom João II

1 Pavilhão do Conhecimento

4

Jardins d'Água

Passeio de Neptuno

For reviews see
◉ Top Experiences	p112
◎ Sights	p115
✕ Eating	p116
☕ Drinking	p117
★ Entertainment	p117
🔒 Shopping	p117

Passeio do Adamastor

14

0 ____ 200 m
0 ____ 0.1 miles

A   B   C   D

Sights

Pavilhão do Conhecimento
MUSEUM

1 MAP P114, C5

At the interactive Pavilhão do Conhecimento, kids can run riot in the adult-free unfinished house, get dizzy on a high-wire bicycle or have fun whipping up tornadoes and blowing massive soap bubbles. (Pavilion of Knowledge; www.pavcon hecimento.pt; Largo José Mariano Gago; adult/child €9/6; 10am-6pm Tue-Fri, 11am-7pm Sat & Sun;)

Torre Vasco da Gama
LANDMARK

2 MAP P114, D1

No, you're not in Dubai! Shaped like the sail of explorer Vasco da Gama's mighty caravel, this 145m-high, concrete-and-steel sky-scraper was designed by architects Leonor Janeiro and Nick Jacobs Sidling up to the tower is the slick, five-star **Myriad by Sana Hotels** (www.myriad.pt; r from €171), which opened in 2013 and bears the hall-mark of architect Nuno Leónidas. Note that the tower is closed to the public, but word has it that Sana is possibly planning a restaurant there. (Cais das Naus)

Teleférico
CABLE CAR

3 MAP P114, D2

Hitch a ride on this 20m-high cable car, linking Torre Vasco da Gama to the Oceanário. The ride affords bird's-eye views across Parque das Nações' skyline and the glittering Rio Tejo that will have you burning up the pixels on your camera. (Telecabine Lisboa; www.telecabinelisboa.pt; Passeio do Tejo; one-way adult/child €3.95/2; 10.30am-8pm Jun–mid-Sep, 11am-6pm or 7pm rest of the year)

Jardins d'Água
WATER PARK

4 MAP P114, C5

These free, themed water gardens are a great spot to cool off in summer. When the sun shines, parents and their overexcited kids get soaked ducking behind the raging waterfalls and misty geysers, and testing out the hands-on water activities. (Water Gardens; www.cm-lisboa.pt/equipamentos/equipamento/info/jardins-da-agua; Rua da Pimenta; 24hr;)

Jardim Garcia de Orta
GARDENS

5 MAP P114, D2

Bristling with exotic foliage from Portugal's former colonies, the Garcia de Orta Garden is named after a 16th-century Portuguese naturalist and pioneer in tropical medicine. Botanical rarities include Madeira's bird of paradise and ser-pentine dragon tree (www.cm-lisboa.pt/equipamentos/equipamento/info/jardim-garcia-de-orta; Rossio dos Olivais; admission free; 24hr;)

Gare do Oriente
ARCHITECTURE

6 MAP P114, B3

Designed by acclaimed Spanish architect Santiago Calatrava, the space-age Gare do Oriente is an extraordinary vaulted structure,

Eat Streets 🍽️

Brazilian, Italian, Indian, Thai, Portuguese – Parque das Nações serves up the world on a plate. Rather than book ahead, you can simply take a stroll along the riverfront and see what grabs you. Restaurants with alfresco seating abound on Passeio das Tágides and Alameda dos Oceanos, many of them offering good-value lunch menus for less than €10. If you're eating on the hoof, try the **Centro Vasco da Gama** (p117) shopping mall, with its snack bars, sushi outlets and cafes.

with slender columns fanning out into a concertina roof to create a kind of geometric crystalline forest. (Oriente Station; Av Dom João II)

Ponte Vasco da Gama BRIDGE

7 ⊙ MAP P106, D1

Vanishing into a watery distance, the Vasco da Gama Bridge is Europe's longest, stretching 17.2km across the Rio Tejo. (www.lusoponte.pt)

Eating

Casa Bota Feijão PORTUGUESE €

8 ✕ MAP P114, B2

Don't be fooled by the nondescript decor and railroad-track views – when a tucked-away place is this crowded with locals at lunchtime

midweek, it must be doing something right. Everyone's here for one thing and one thing only: Bairrada-style *leitão* – suckling pig spit-roasted on an open fire until juicy and meltingly tender, doused in a beautiful peppery garlic sauce. (📞 218 532 489; www.restaurantebotafeijao.pt; Rua Conselheiro Lopo Vaz 5; half/whole portions €8.50/12; 🕗 8am-8pm Mon-Fri)

ZeroZero PIZZA €€

9 ✕ MAP P114, C4

This location of top pizzeria ZeroZero is a modern, industrial-chic affair. Inside, a massive wall of firewood fuels the wood-burning ovens, which churn out favourites like 18-month prosciutto *de parma* with mushrooms or *fior di latte* mozzarella, porcini, asiago cheese and black truffle cream. Outside, a large and airy patio is a fine retreat from Parque das Nações. (📞 218 957 016; www.pizzeriazerozero.pt; Alameda dos Oceanos; pizza €9.50-18.50; 🕗 noon-midnight Sun-Thu, to 1am Fri & Sat; 🛜)

Old House CHINESE €€€

10 ✕ MAP P114, D3

Transport yourself to China at this authentic Szechuan power-house (tamed for local tastes), an upscale Chinese chain restaurant that chose Parque das Nações for its first foray outside the motherland. (📞 218 969 075; www.theoldhouseportugal.pt; Rua Pimenta 9; mains €9.90-45; 🕗 noon-3pm & 7pm-midnight; 🛜)

River Lounge   MEDITERRANEAN €€€

11 ✖ MAP P114, D1

This slinky, monochrome, glass-walled restaurant-lounge has upped the style ante in Parque das Nações. Seasonal, Med-inspired cuisine is given a light touch of sophistication in dishes such as roasted lobster with winter fruit vol-au-vent and curried pear, or half-cured cod with salt-cured tuna (*muxuma*), celery purée, squid ink and asparagus. (🖉211 107 600; www.myriad.pt; Cais das Naus, Myriad by Sana Hotels; mains €19-48; ⏲restaurant 12.30-3.30pm & 7.30-10pm, bar 9.30am-2am; 🛜)

Drinking

Fábrica Coffee Truck   COFFEE

12 ☕ MAP P114, B3

Inside a vintage Citroën HY panel van near the main exit of Gare do Oriente, you'll find some of Lisbon's best third-wave coffee – proprietarily roasted single-origin arabica beans from Brazil, Ethiopia and Colombia, prepared by properly trained baristas. (www.fabricacoffeeroasters.com; Av Dom João II, Gare do Oriente; ⏲8am-5pm Mon-Fri, 9-1pm Sat)

Irish & Co   IRISH PUB

13 ☕ MAP P114, D2

This double-decker chain pub is the liveliest drinking den along the waterfront. There's typical homesick-remedying pub fare, and several beers, including Guinness, Kilkenny, Carlsberg and several of Super Bock's more crafty attempts,

are on draught. A suspended biplane hovers above the large patio (though water views are partially blocked by shrubbery). (www.grupodocadesanto.com.pt; Rua Pimenta 57; ⏲noon-2am Sun-Wed, to 3am Thu-Sat; 🛜)

Entertainment

Teatro Camões   BALLET

14 ✪ MAP P114, C6

Teatro Camões is home to the Portuguese National Ballet Company, which is under the artistic direction of Paulo Ribeiro. (🖉218 923 477; www.cnb.pt/teatro-camoes; Passeio do Neptuno; ⏲box office 1-5pm Nov-Apr, 2-6pm May-Oct)

Shopping

Oceanário de Lisboa Store   GIFTS & SOUVENIRS

15 🔒 MAP P114, C4

The Oceanário's 600-sq-metre ecofocused museum shop stocks clothes, souvenirs, cuddly toys and more, and has partnerships with local producers and craft workers. (www.oceanario.pt; Esplanada Dom Carlos I, Oceanário; ⏲10am-8pm, to 7pm in winter)

Centro Vasco da Gama   MALL

16 🔒 MAP P114, C3

A glass-roofed mall sheltering high-street stores, a cinema and food court – upper-level restaurants have outdoor seating with views. (www.centrovascodagama.pt; Av D João II 40; ⏲9am-midnight)

Explore ⊕
Marquês de Pombal, Rato & Saldanha

Some of Lisbon's finest restaurants, designer boutiques and concert halls will fill an entire day in this northern swath. Beyond the tree-fringed Avenida da Liberdade lie graceful art-nouveau houses, manicured gardens and galleries showcasing artists from Paula Rego to Rembrandt.

The Short List

○ **Museu Calouste Gulbenkian – Coleção do Fundador (p120)** *Ogle a world-class collection of epic Western and Eastern art at this outstanding art museum.*

○ **Casa-Museu Medeiros e Almeida (p124)** *One of Europe's best private collections of timepieces, Ming and Qing dynasty porcelain.*

○ **Mãe d'Água (p124)** *Wander part of the city's astonishing 18th-century aqueduct system.*

○ **Red Frog (p128)** *A sophisticated world of mixology lies behind the signless Red Frog.*

Getting There & Around

Ⓜ Attractions are spread out but the metro is a breeze. Handy stops on the yellow and blue lines: Avenida, Marquês de Pombal, Rato, São Sebastião and Parque. If you're visiting more than one place, invest in a 24-hour Carris/metro pass.

🚌 The Aero stops at Marquês de Pombal and Avenida da Liberdade en route to and from Lisbon's airport.

Neighbourhood Map on p122

Praça Marquês de Pombal GUSTAVO FRAZAO/SHUTTERSTOCK ©

Top Experience 📷

See the Epic Art Collection of Museu Calouste Gulbenkian

This epic collection of Western and Eastern art is famous for its outstanding quality and breadth. You can easily spend half a day taking a chronological tour of the treasures that wealthy Armenian art collector Calouste Sarkis Gulbenkian (1869–1955) picked up on his world travels – this is an exuberant feast of fine and decorative arts.

◉ MAP P122, C1

www.gulbenkian.pt

Av de Berna 45A

Coleção do Fundador/ Coleção Moderna combo ticket adult/child €11.50/ free, Sun free from 2pm

🕙 10am-6pm Wed-Mon

Dutch & Flemish Masters

Old Master enthusiasts are in their element contemplating 17th-century masterpieces such as Rembrandt's chiaroscuro *Portrait of an Old Man* and Rubens' frantic *Loves of the Centaurs* and biblical *Flight into Egypt*. Ruisdael's stormy Norwegian scenes and van Dyck portraits star among other highlights.

René Lalique

An entire room spotlights the impossibly intricate glassware and jewellery of French art-nouveau designer René Lalique. Marvel at his naturalistic diadems, hair combs, chalices and bracelets, bejewelled with baroque pearls and opals.

19th-Century Fine Art

This collection zooms in on French and English masterpieces such as Manet's *Boy Blowing Bubbles*, Monet's *Break-Up of the Ice* and Turner's *Wreck of a Transport Ship*. Look, too, for Impressionistic Degas portraits, Théodore Rousseau landscapes and Rodin's *Eternal Spring* sculpture.

Egyptian & Greco-Roman Art

With its gilded mummy mask, bronze cats and bas-relief pharaohs, the Egyptian collection provides a fascinating insight into this chapter of history. Next is the Greco-Roman room, displaying Greek coins and medallions, Roman glass and ceramics.

Islamic Art

Be captivated by the rich hues and geometric patterns of the museum's Persian carpets, kilims and brocaded silk – many dating to the 15th and 16th centuries. These feature alongside Ottoman faience, ornate tiles and Egyptian mosque lamps.

★ Top Tips

○ Visit on Sunday after 2pm when entry to the permanent collection is free.

○ Guided English tours (€12) run on Sunday and Monday at 11am.

○ Check the website for special events aimed at kids and families.

○ Learn more about the works on display with an audio guide.

✕ Take a Break

For something sweet, take a stroll to nearby Versailles (p126), a gloriously old-world patisserie.

The food court Gourmet Experience (p126) at El Corte Inglés dishes up fantastic and quick meals from Michelin-starred Iberian chefs, including José Avillez and Henrique Sá Pessoa.

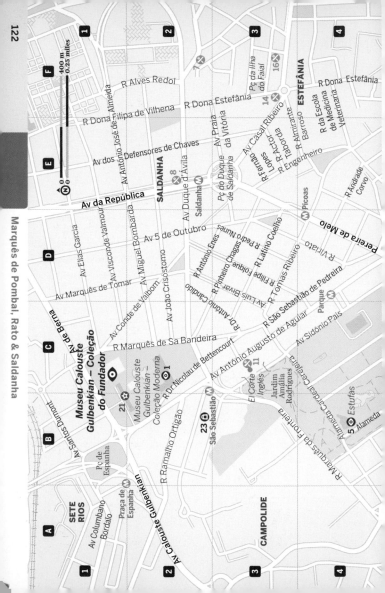

400 m
0.25 miles

SETE RIOS

Av Columbano Bordalo

Av Santos Dumont

Pç de Espanha

Praça de Espanha

Av Calouste Gulbenkian

R Ramalho Ortigão

Av de Berna

Museu Calouste Gulbenkian – Coleção do Fundador

21

Museu Calouste Gulbenkian – Coleção Moderna

1

R Dr Nicolau de Bettencourt

23

São Sebastião

CAMPOLIDE

El Corte Inglés

Jardim Amália Rodrigues

11

R Marquês da Fronteira

Av António Augusto de Aguiar

Estufas

5

Alameda

Av Elias Garcia

Av Visconde Valmor

Av Marquês de Tomar

Av Miguel Bombarda

Av Conde de Valbom

R Dr António Candido

Av João Crisóstomo

Av 5 de Outubro

R António Enes

R Pinheiro Chagas

R Filipe Folque

R Pedro Nunes

Av Luís Bivar

R Filipe Coelho

R Latino Coelho

R Tomás Ribeiro

R São Sebastião de Pedreira

Av Sidónio Pais

Parque

Pereira de Melo

Picoas

R Virato

R Andrade Corvo

Av da República

Av Duque d'Ávila

SALDANHA

8

Saldanha

Pç do Duque de Saldanha

Av dos Defensores de Chaves

Av António José de Almeida

R Dona Filipa de Vilhena

R Alves Redol

R Dona Almeida

R Dona Estefânia

Av Praia da Vitória

Av Casal Ribeiro

R Fernão Lopes

R Actor Taborda

R Almirante Barroso

R Engenheiro

Pç da Ilha do Faial

ESTEFÂNIA

R Dona Estefânia

R da Escola de Medicina Veterinária

7

16

14

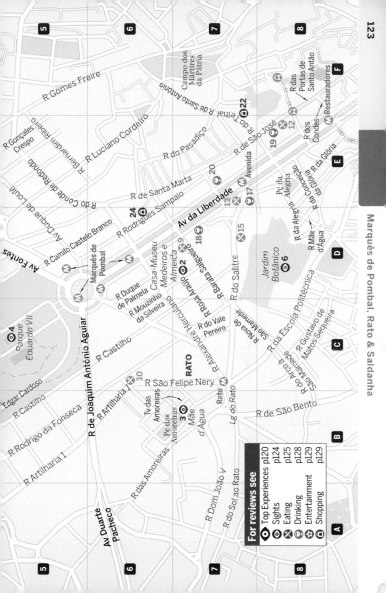

5
6
7
8

R Gomes Freire

R Gonçalves Crespo

R Bernardim Ribeiro

R Luciano Cordeiro

R do Conde de Redondo

R do Pasadiço

Av Duque de Loulé

R de Santa Marta

R do Telhal R de Santo António

Campo dos Mártires da Pátria

22

R de São José

R das Portas de Santo Antão

19 **12**

F

M Restauradores

R dos Condes

M Avenida

20

R de Rodrigues Sampaio

24

Av da Liberdade

13 **17**

Pç da Alegria

R da Alegria R da Glória

M

R da Conceição da Glória

E

R Mãe d'Água

Av Fontes

R Camilo Castelo Branco

Marquês de Pombal M

M Marquês de Pombal M

M

R Duque de Palmela

Casa-Museu Medeiros e Almeida

R Mouzinho da Silveira

R Rosa Araújo

9

2

18

R Barata Salgueiro

15

R do Salitre

Jardim Botânico

6

R da Escola Politécnica

D

4

Parque Eduardo VII

Edgar Cardoso

R Castilho

R Rodrigo da Fonseca

R Castilho

R do Vale Pereiro

R Alexandre Herculano

R Nova de São Mamede

R Gustavo de Matos Sequeira

R do Arco a São Mamede

C

R de Joaquim António Aguiar

10

R Artilharia 1

R São Felipe Nery

Tv das Amoreiras

Pç das Amoreiras

3

Mãe d'Água

RATO

M Rato

Lg do Rato

R de São Bento

B

R Artilharia 1

R das Amoreiras

Av Duarte Pacheco

R Dom João V

R do Sol ao Rato

A

For reviews see
◉ Top Experiences p120
◉ Sights p124
✗ Eating p125
◎ Drinking p128
◻ Entertainment p129
◻ Shopping p129

5
6
7
8

Sights

Museu Calouste Gulbenkian – Coleção Moderna
MUSEUM

1 MAP P122, C2

Situated in a sculpture-dotted garden, the Coleção Moderna reveals a stellar collection of 20th-century Portuguese and international art. (Modern Collection; www.gulbenkian.pt; Av de Berna 45A; Coleção Moderna/Coleção do Fundador combo ticket adult/child €11.50/free, temporary exhibitions €3-6, Sun free from 2pm; ⏲10am-6pm Wed-Mon)

Casa-Museu Medeiros e Almeida
MUSEUM

2 MAP P122, D7

Housed in a stunning early-19th-century mansion, this little-known museum presents António Medeiros e Almeida's exquisite fine- and decorative-arts collection. Highlights include Han ceramics and Ming- and Qing-dynasty porcelain, Thomas Gainsborough paintings, a 300-strong stockpile

Free Museum & Gallery Entry

Save museum and gallery visits for the weekend. The Museu Calouste Gulbenkian museums (Coleção do Fundador and Coleção Moderna) both offer free entry on Sunday after 2pm, while the Casa-Museu Medeiros e Almeida is gratis from 10am to 1pm on Saturday.

of watches and clocks, and a dinner service that once belonged to Napoléon Bonaparte. (www.casa-museumedeirosealmeida.pt; Rua Rosa Araújo 41; adult/child €5/free, free 10am-1pm Sat; ⏲10am-5pm Mon-Sat)

Mãe d'Água
HISTORIC BUILDING

3 MAP P122, B7

The king laid the aqueduct's final stone at Mãe d'Água, the city's massive 5500-cu-metre main reservoir. Completed in 1834, the reservoir's cool, echoing chamber is a fine place to admire 19th-century technology. Climb the stairs for a fine view of the aqueduct and the surrounding neighbourhood. Admission is €5 if there's an exhibition on. (Mother of Water; www.epal.pt; Praça das Amoreiras 10; adult/child €3/1.50, Sun free; ⏲10am-12.30pm & 1.30-5.30pm Tue-Sun)

Parque Eduardo VII
PARK

4 MAP P122, C5

An urban oasis with British roots, Parque Eduardo VII is named after his highness Edward VII, who visited Lisbon in 1903. The sloping parterre affords sweeping views over the whizzing traffic of Praça Marquês de Pombal to the river. (Alameda Edgar Cardoso; admission free; ⏲24hr)

Estufas
GARDENS

5 MAP P122, B4

Tucked away in a pocket of Parque Eduardo VII, this trio of glasshouses nurtures tree ferns and camellias

Mãe d'Água

in the *estufa fría* (cool greenhouse), coffee and mango trees in the *estufa quente* (hot greenhouse) and cacti in the *estufa doce* (sweet greenhouse). (Greenhouses; http://estufafria.cm-lisboa.pt; Parque Eduardo VII; adult/child €3.10/2.33, free Sun 9am-2pm; ⏰10am-7pm Apr-Oct, 9am-5pm Nov-Mar)

Jardim Botânico   GARDENS

6 ◎ MAP P122, D8

Nurtured by green-fingered students, the Jardim Botânico is a quiet, 1500-species pocket of lushness fresh off a €500,000 renovation that mostly improved infrastructure but also included a new amphitheatre. Look out for Madeiran geraniums, sequoias, purple jacarandas and, by the entrance (upper-level gardens), a gigantic Moreton Bay fig tree. It's also worth a peek inside the butterfly house. (Botanical Garden; www.mnhnc.ulisboa.pt; Rua da Escola Politécnica 58; adult/child €2/1; ⏰gardens 9am-8pm, butterfly house 10am-5pm Tue-Fri, 11am-6pm Sat & Sun)

Eating

Tasca Fit   HEALTH FOOD €

7 ✕ MAP P122, F2

Spacious and brightly decorated, this restaurant serves affordable, healthy, sugar-free food, served in generous portions. It's one of the few in the area serving vegetarian options and Brazilian-style crêpe-like tapioca offerings. (www.tascafit.pt; Rua Visconde de Santarém 69B; mains €6-12; ⏰8am-11pm Mon-Fri, 11am-2am Sat; ❄🖉)

Versailles
PASTRIES €

8 ✖ MAP P122, E2

With a marble chandelier and icing-sugar stucco confection, this sublime patisserie is where well-coiffed ladies come to gossip and devour cream cakes, espresso with *sortidos Húngaros* (chocolate-covered cookies) and house-spawned chocolate cake (served disc-shaped; it's oh, so decadent!). (Av da República 15A; pastries €0.85-2.30; ☺7.30am-11.45pm; 🛜)

Avenida SushiCafé
JAPANESE €€

9 ✖ MAP P122, D7

Don't let the flagship location of what is essentially a mall-food-court sushi chain fool you: Chef Daniel Rente creates some surprisingly and seriously good Japanese fusion food. (📞211 928 158; www.sushicafe.pt; Rua Barata Salgueiro 28; tasting menu €65, dishes €4.80-22; ☺12.30-4.30pm & 6-10pm Mon-Wed, to 1am Thu & Fri, 12.30pm-1am Sat; 🛜)

Forno d'Oro
PIZZA €€

10 ✖ MAP P122, C6

True to its name, Lisbon's most serious pizzeria indeed produces pies out of a golden (brick) oven. The burrata and buffalo mozzarella here is flown in daily from Italy, and pizzas feature PDO-protected ingredients from the motherland. Seasonal specials shake up the status quo. (📞213 879 944; www.fornodoro.pt; Rua Artilharia 1 16B; pizza €10.50-19.95; ☺noon-3pm & 7-11pm; 🛜)

Gourmet Experience
FOOD HALL €€

11 ✖ MAP P122, C3

The previously underused 7th floor of Lisbon's fanciest department store was transformed into the Gourmet Experience in late 2017. A supersized version of a gourmet food hall idea imported from Madrid, this high-end food court with table service is a culinary cornucopia of top Lisboan and Iberian chefs. (www.elcorteingles.pt/gourmet-experience; Av António Augusto de Aguiar 31, El Corte Inglés; mains €8-27.50; ☺10am-midnight Sun-Thu, to 1am Fri & Sat; 🛜)

Jesus é Goês
INDIAN €€

12 ✖ MAP P122, E8

At one of Lisbon's best Indian restaurants, jovial chef Jesus Lee whips up contemporary Goan delicacies. Rice-sack tablecloths and colourful murals set the scene for starters such as onion-coriander chickpea fritters or potato bhaji with puri, followed by mushroom and chestnut or shrimp curries, or 11-spices goat – all fiery-fantastic. Reserve ahead. Cash only. (📞211 545 812; Rua de São José 23; mains €8-18.50; ☺noon-3pm & 7-11pm Tue-Sat; 🛜)

Cervejaria Ribadouro
SEAFOOD €€

13 ✖ MAP P122, E7

Bright, noisy and full to the gills, this bustling beer hall is popular with local seafood fans, some

Aqueduct of the Free Waters

👍

The 109 arches of the **Aqueduto das Águas Livres** lope across the hills into Lisbon from Caneças, more than 18km away; they are most spectacular at Campolide, where the tallest arch is an incredible 65m high. Built between 1728 and 1835, by order of Dom João V, the aqueduct is a spectacular feat of engineering and brought Lisbon its first clean drinking water. Its more sinister claim to fame is as the site where 19th-century mass murderer Diogo Alves pushed his victims over the edge. No prizes for guessing why it was closed to the public soon after.

of whom just belly up to the bar, chase their fresh shrimp and *tremoços* (lupin beans) with an ice-cold *imperial* (draught beer) and call it a night. The shellfish are plucked fresh from the tank, weighed and cooked to lip-smacking perfection. (📞 213 549 411; www.cervejariaribadouro.pt; Rua do Salitre 2; mains €11-30, seafood per kg €42.50-147; ⏱ noon-1.30am; 🛜)

Zaafran
INDIAN €€

14 🍽 MAP P122, F3

Mozambican-raised Indians run this subcontinental gem near Saldanha, an affordable option in the area and an alternative to the nearby shopping centre's food courts. The lunch *thalis* are authentic (from €9.90), the accompanying salsas are legit hot, and Mozambican influences, especially in the prawn dishes and specials like peanut curries, shake things up enough that the menu is nontraditional Indian. (📞 213 558 894; Largo Dona Estefânia 7; mains

€9-17.50; ⏱ noon-3pm & 7.30-11pm Mon-Sat; 🛜)

Os Tibetanos
VEGETARIAN €€

15 🍽 MAP P122, D7

Lisbon's oldest herbivore temple is part of a Tibetan Buddhism school. Its mantra is fresh vegetarian food, with daily specials such as quiche and curry. Sit in the serene courtyard if the sun's out and save room for the rose-petal ice cream. (📞 213 142 038; www.tibetanos.com; Rua do Salitre 117; mains €10-13; ⏱ 12.15-2.45pm & 7.30-10.30pm Sun-Fri, 12.30-3.30pm & 8-11pm Sat; 🛜 🍴)

Horta dos Brunos
PORTUGUESE €€€

16 🍽 MAP P122, F3

Chef Pedro Filipe's somewhat unknown and unassuming gourmet *tasca*, a favourite among moving and shaking politicians and in-the-know gastronauts, does some of Lisbon's best work. There's a menu, but stick to your server's rundown of what's cooking daily, such as extraordinary tuna, cuttlefish *à lagareiro* and succulent lamb chops, all beautifully presented and modern in execution. There are top-end French wines, too. (☎ 213 153 421; Rua Ilha do Pico 27; mains €25-30; ☺ noon-3pm & 7-11pm Mon-Sat)

Drinking

Red Frog   COCKTAIL BAR

17 🚇 MAP P122, E7

In true speakeasy fashion, Red Frog is accessed via a 'Press for Cocktails' doorbell and a list of rules. Enter a sophisticated mixology world of craft cocktails and appropriate glassware, dress and behaviour. (www.facebook.com/redfrogspeakeasy; Rua do Salitre 5A; ☺ 6pm-2am Mon-Thu, to 3am Fri & Sat)

Sky Bar   BAR

18 🚇 MAP P122, D7

Wow, what a view! This high-rise bar at the Tivoli has a gorgeous terrace, full of minimalist white nooks for sipping expensive cocktails (€12 to €17), conversing and drinking in the panorama of Lisbon. (www.skybarrooftop.com; Av da Liberdade 185, 9th fl, Hotel Tivoli Lisboa; ☺ 5pm-1am Apr-Sep, 4pm-midnight Oct-Mar)

La Ronera   BAR

19 🚇 MAP P122, E8

Some fun Venezuelan expats run this minuscule bar that showers a whole lotta Latin love on a somewhat obscure spirit from Lisbon's perspective – the rum that flows here is not only from

Avenida da Liberdade

Venezuela but from all over Central and South America, the Caribbean and beyond. (www.facebook.com/laroneralx; Rua de São José 43; ⏰5pm-midnight Mon-Thu, to 2am Fri & Sat)

JNêQUOI Delibar COCKTAIL BAR

20 📍 MAP P122, E7

A lavish bar fit for its chic address, this drinking den below the upscale restaurant of the same name caters to a well-heeled crowd who gather around the long, contorted marble bar to chase cold bar delicacies (fresh oysters, caviar) with exquisite spirits. (www.jncquoi.com; Av da Liberdade 182-184; ⏰10am-midnight Sun-Wed, to 2am Thu-Sat; 🤖)

Entertainment

Fundação Calouste Gulbenkian CLASSICAL MUSIC, BALLET

21 ⭐ MAP P122, B1

Home to the Gulbenkian Orchestra, this classical-music heavyweight stages first-rate concerts and ballets. (📞217 823 000; www.gulbenkian.pt; Av de Berna 45A)

Shopping

Carbono MUSIC

22 🏷 MAP P122, F7

The staff may be grumpy, but it's hard not to like Carbono, with its impressive selection of new and second-hand vinyl and CDs. World music is especially well represented. (www.carbono.com.pt; Rua do Telhal 6B; ⏰11am-7pm Mon-Sat)

Exploring the Avenida

The tree-fringed 19th-century Avenida da Liberdade is a 1100m-long ribbon of style, linking Praça dos Restauradores in the south to busy Marquês de Pombal roundabout in the north. This is Lisbon's classic strolling boulevard, flanked by some of the city's choicest hotels, cafes and designer boutiques.

House of Eleh SHOES

23 🏷 MAP P122, B2

Eleh is one of the world's oldest makers of women's shoes (from €200), knocking out exquisitely handcrafted footwear since 1840. Today, eighth-generation cobbler Helena Amante runs the show, producing culturally themed, limited-edition kicks like Indo-Portuguese-patterned summer flats and winter boots wrapped in Alentejan *manta* (a blanket-like material), among others. (📞211 922 424; www.eleh.eu; Av Ressano Garcia 11F; ⏰by appointment)

Fátima Lopes FASHION & ACCESSORIES

24 🏷 MAP P122, D6

Fátima's has an immaculate collection of Latin-inspired threads, from slinky suits to itsy-glitzy prom dresses and hot-pink ball gowns. (📞213 240 550; www.fatimalopes.com; Rua Rodrigues Sampaio 96; ⏰9am-6pm Mon-Fri)

Explore ◈
Estrela, Lapa & Alcântara

In quiet, tree-lined Estrela and Lapa you can easily tiptoe off the well-trodden trail along cafe-rimmed squares, lanes with breezy river views and gentrified streets where 18th-century mansions harbour antique stores, boutiques and galleries. Down by the river, Alcântara signals a new age for Lisbon: its once-industrial warehouses have been reborn as en-vogue bars, clubs and restaurants.

○ **Basílica da Estrela (p136)** Marvelling at this 1790 neoclassical basilica, including the stunning presépio and expansive rooftop views over Lisbon.

○ **Museu da Marioneta (p136)** Discovering your inner child at this enchanting puppet museum.

○ **Museu Nacional de Arte Antiga (p132)** Wandering the hallowed halls in this world-class museum set inside a 17th-century palace.

○ **Museu do Oriente (p137)** Admiring priceless Asian antiquities in this museum occupying a revamped 1940s bacalhau (dried salt-cod) warehouse.

Getting There & Around

🚊 Tram 15E from Praça da Figueira and 18E from Cais do Sodré reach Santos and Alcântara. Tram 25 trundles to Santos, Lapa and Estrela. 28E is also convenient for Estrela.

🚌 Buses 713 (Arco do Cego–Estação Campolide) and 727 (Estação Roma–Areeiro–Restelo) stop in Estrela, Lapa and Alcântara. 712 is useful for Alcântara.

Neighbourhood Map on p134

Jardim da Estrela (p136) RADU BERCAN/SHUTTERSTOCK ©

Top Experience 📷
Tour a Palace of Art at the Museu Nacional de Arte Antiga

On its scenic perch above the river, this 17th-century palace is a grand backdrop for Lisbon's foremost ancient-art collection. And what a collection! Meissen porcelain, Portuguese sculpture, Beauvais tapestry, Ming porcelain, baroque silverware and Japanese screens do a stellar job of whisking you through the world of fine and decorative arts from the Middle Ages to the 19th century.

◉ MAP P134, E4

National Museum of Ancient Art

www.museudearteantiga.pt

Rua das Janelas Verdes

adult/child €6/free, with themed exhibitions €10/free

🕐 10am-6pm Tue-Sun

Panels of St Vincent

Covering an entire wall (room 12; 3rd floor), the *Panels of St Vincent* are the museum's pride and joy. Attributed to Nuno Gonçalves, the painter of King Afonso V, and dating to 1470, the expressive polyptych depicts the veneration of St Vincent.

Monstrance & Cross

The gold and silverware collection's two stand-outs hide in room 29. First up is Gil Vicente's golden wonder, the Monstrance of Belém (1506), made from the gold brought back from Vasco da Gama's second voyage to India, and embellished with armillary spheres and the 12 Apostles. Just as dazzling is the 1214 processional cross of King Sancho I, delicately engraved and bejewelled with pearls and sapphires.

European Painting

Strong on ecclesiastical painting, this collection takes a blockbuster tour of 14th- to 19th-century European art. Two pieces in particular stand out. The first is a Renaissance masterpiece, Albrecht Dürer's chiaroscuro *St Jerome* (1521). The second is Hieronymus Bosch's devotional triptych, *St Anthony* (1500), an evocative depiction of the hermit being attacked by demons and faced with sins like gluttony and abandonment of the faith.

Oriental Art & Ceramics

Exquisite 16th-century Indian caskets inlaid with mother of pearl, Ming porcelain and geometric tiles from Syria and Turkey all beg exploration on the 2nd floor. Be sure to see the beautifully gilded Namban screens, depicting the arrival of the Namban (southern barbarians), the Portuguese explorers who arrived in Japan in 1543 and shocked locals with their uncouth behaviour.

★ Top Tips

o This museum is simply huge, so pick up a map at the entrance to pinpoint what you really want to see. Allow a minimum of two hours.

o Arrive early or late to dodge the crowds.

o Biannual temporary themed exhibitions (priced separately, at around €6) are reached via a second entrance on Rua das Janelas Verdes.

✕ Take a Break

Step next door to Le Chat (p140) for drinks and snacks on the terrace with captivating river views.

Quimera Brewpub (p140), 800m west, does craft beer and cocktails inside a cinematic, stone-walled 18th-century carriage tunnel.

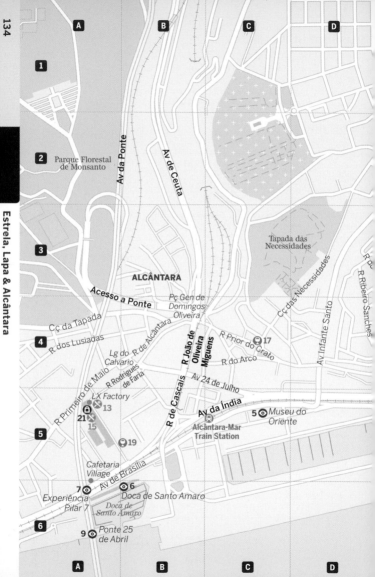

A
B
C
D

1

2 Parque Florestal
de Monsanto

Av da Ponte

Av de Ceuta

3

Tapada das
Necessidades

ALCÂNTARA

Acesso a Ponte

Pç Gen de
Domingos
Oliveira

R do Ribeiro Sanches

Cç das Necessidades

Av Infante Santo

4 Cç da Tapada
R dos Lusiadas

Lg do
Calvario

R de Alcântara

R João de
Oliveira
Miguens

R Prior do Crato 17

R do Arco

Av 24 de Julho

R Rodrigues
de Faria

R Primeiro de Maio

LX Factory

21 13

R de Cascais

Av da Índia

5 Museu do
Oriente

5
15

19

Alcântara-Mar
Train Station

Cafetaria
Village

Av de Brasília

7 6

Experiência
Pilar 7

Doca de Santo Amaro

Doca de
Santo Amaro

6

9 Ponte 25
de Abril

A
B
C
D

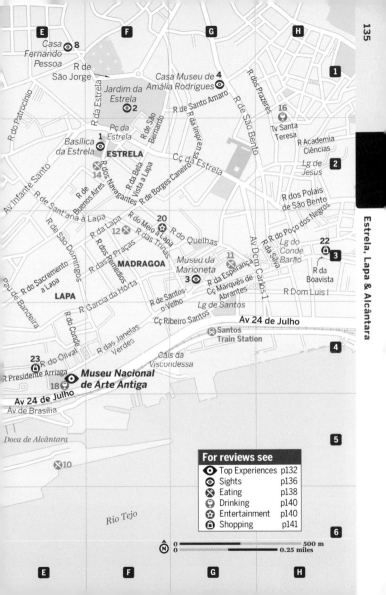

E

F

G

H

E8 Casa Fernando Pessoa

R de São Jorge

R da Estrela

F

Jardim da Estrela **2**

G Casa Museu de Amália Rodrigues **4**

R de Santo Amaro

R de São Bernardo

R da Imprensa à Estrela

R de São Bento

R dos Prazeres

H

16 Tv Santa Teresa

R Academia Ciências

2 Lg de Jesus

Basílica da Estrela **1**

ESTRELA

Pç da Estrela

R de São Bento

Cç da Estrela

14

R dos Navagantes

R da Bela Vista à Lapa

R de Borges Caneiro

R dos Polais de São Bento

R de Buenos Aires

R de Sant'ana à Lapa

Av Infante Santo

20

R do Meio à Lapa

R do Quelhas

Av Dom Carlos 1

R da Silva

R do Poço dos Negros

R do Conde Barão

22 **3**

12 R da Lapa

R das Trinas

R dos Remédios

R das Praças

MADRAGOA

Museu da Marioneta **3**

11

R da Esperança

Cç Marquês de Abrantes

R da Boavista

R Dom Luis I

R de São Domingos

Pau de R de Sacramento à Lapa

LAPA

R Garcia da Horta

R das Janelas Verdes

R de Santos-o-Velho

Lg de Santos

Pau de Bandeira

R do Conde

Cais da Viscondessa

Cç Ribeiro Santos

Av 24 de Julho

Santos Train Station

4

23 R do Olival

R Presidente Arriaga

18

Museu Nacional de Arte Antiga

Av 24 de Julho

Av de Brasília

Doca de Alcântara

5

10

Rio Tejo

For reviews see

◉	Top Experiences	p132
◉	Sights	p136
✖	Eating	p138
🍷	Drinking	p140
★	Entertainment	p140
🛍	Shopping	p141

N

0 ————— 500 m
0 ————— 0.25 miles

6

E

F

G

H

Sights

Basílica da Estrela

CHURCH

1 ⊙ MAP P134, F2

The curvaceous, sugar-white dome and twin belfries of Basílica da Estrela are visible from afar. The echoing interior is awash with pink-and-black marble, which creates a kaleidoscopic effect when you gaze up into the cupola. The neoclassical beauty was completed in 1790 by order of Dona Maria I (whose tomb is here) in gratitude for a male heir. (Praça da Estrela; basilica free, nativity scene €2, roof €3; ⊙basilica 9.30am-1pm & 3-7.30pm, terrace 10am-6.40pm, presépio 10-11.30am & 3-5pm, closed Mon, Sat & Sun morning, Wed afternoon)

Jardim da Estrela

GARDENS

2 ⊙ MAP P134, F1

Seeking green respite? Opposite the Basílica da Estrela, this 1852 green space is perfect for a stroll, with paths weaving past pine, monkey-puzzle and palm trees, rose and cacti beds, and the centrepiece – a giant banyan tree. Kids love the duck ponds and animal-themed playground. There are several open-air cafes where you can recharge. (Praça da Estrela; admission free; ⊙7am-midnight; ▦)

Museu da Marioneta

MUSEUM

3 ⊙ MAP P134, G3

Discover your inner child at the surprisingly enchanting Museu da Marioneta, a veritable Geppetto's

Doca de Santo Amaro

workshop housed in the 17th-century Convento das Bernardas. Alongside superstars such as impish Punch and his Portuguese equivalent Dom Roberto are rarities: Vietnamese water puppets, Sicilian opera marionettes and intricate Burmese shadow puppets. Check out the fascinating exhibit of the making of the animation film *A Suspeita*. (Puppet Museum; www.museudamarioneta.pt; Rua da Esperança 146; adult/child €5/3, free before noon Sun; ⏱10am-6pm Tue-Sun; ⍟)

Casa Museu de Amália Rodrigues
MUSEUM

4 ◉ MAP P134, G1

A pilgrimage site for fado fans, Casa Museu de Amália Rodrigues is where the Rainha do Fado (Queen of Fado) Amália Rodrigues lived; note the *calçada portuguesa* (Portuguese sidewalk design) announcing 'Amália'. Short tours take in portraits, glittering costumes and crackly recordings of her performances. (www.amaliarodrigues.pt; Rua de São Bento 193; adult/child under 5yr €6/free; ⏱10am-6pm)

Museu do Oriente
MUSEUM

5 ◉ MAP P134, C5

The beautifully designed Museu do Oriente highlights Portugal's ties with Asia, from colonial baby steps in Macau to ancestor worship. The cavernous museum occupies a revamped 1940s *bacalhau* (dried salt-cod) warehouse – a €30-million conversion. Strikingly displayed in pitch-black rooms,

Waterfront Walkabout

One of Lisbon's best and most atmospheric spots for a stroll stretches from Torre de Belém to Doca de Santo Amaro (and beyond) – a leisurely 4km promenade hugging the Rio Tejo. Join *lisboêtas* with a cocktail or an ice cream and lap up the local colour along this festive esplanade.

the permanent collection focuses on the Portuguese presence in Asia, and Asian gods. (www.museudooriente.pt; Doca de Alcântara; adult/child €6/2, free 6-10pm Fri; ⏱10am-6pm Tue-Thu, Sat & Sun, to 10pm Fri)

Doca de Santo Amaro
LANDMARK

6 ◉ MAP P134, B6

This group of old warehouses have been converted into a lovely patch of restaurants and bars, all with stupendous views over the marina and Ponte 25 de Abril.

Experiência Pilar 7
VIEWPOINT

7 ◉ MAP P134, A6

Experiência Pilar 7 affords the opportunity to get up close and personal with the iconic Ponte 25 de Abril (p138) from 80m above ground. The €5.3-million attraction, opened in late 2017, includes a walk-through multimedia tour of the Golden Gate–lookalike bridge

Double-Decker Dining 🍽

An offshoot of what was originally a London cultural project, Village Underground Lisboa is hidden inside the Carris complex in Alcântara. The multiuse space houses the fun **Cafetaria Village** (Map p134, A6; www.vulisboa. com; Rua Primeiro de Maio 103, Village Underground Lisboa; mains €3.50-8; ⏱noon-8pm Apr-Sep, to 6pm Tue-Sun Oct-Mar; 🛜👪), located inside a raised antique double-decker city bus resting on shipping containers (great for kids). Most tourists don't wander in here, despite it being visible (though not accessible) from Avenida Brasília and Ponte 25 de Abril.

that's a real treat for engineering buffs, particularly the (vertigo-inducing) transition between the suspended metal bridge and the concrete viaduct, and the fascinating twin rooms where the main moorings of the support cables are visible. Kids will also be impressed. (www.visitlisboa.com; Ponte 25 de Abril; adult/child €6/free; ⏱10am-6pm Oct-Apr, to 8pm May-Sep)

Casa Fernando Pessoa   CULTURAL CENTRE

8 ⊙ MAP P134, E1

Immerse yourself in the life and work of Portuguese modernist founder and author Fernando

Pessoa as you wander through his old apartment, browse through his book collection (digitised), attempt to decipher some of his handwritten notes, and admire paintings and tapestries of the author by fellow members of the movement, such as painter Júlio Pomar. (📞213 913 270; www.casafernandopessoa.pt; Rua Coelho da Rocha 16; adult/child/guided tour €3/free/4; ⏱10am-6pm Mon-Sat, guided tours in English 11.30am Mon, Fri & Sat)

Ponte 25 de Abril   BRIDGE

9 ⊙ MAP P134, A6

Most people experience visual déjà vu the first time they clap eyes on the bombastic suspension bridge Ponte 25 de Abril. It's hardly surprising given that it's the spitting image of San Francisco's Golden Gate Bridge, was constructed by the same company in 1966 and, at 2.27km, is almost as long. (www. lusoponte.pt; Doca de Santo Amaro)

Eating

Último Porto   SEAFOOD €€

10 🍴 MAP P134, E5

An absolute local's secret for a reason, this top seafooder takes an act of God to find. Hidden among the shipping-container cranes of the Port of Lisbon, fantastically simple grilled fish paired with top Alentejan and Douro wines draw locals in droves. With shipping containers and departmental port buildings framing the ambience, María do Céu oversees a parking-lot-style grill. (📞308 808 939; Estação Marítima da Rocha do Conde de Óbidos; mains €8.50-17; ⏰8am-4.30pm Mon-Sat)

Petiscaria Ideal

FUSION €€

11 🍴 MAP P134, G3

This small, buzzing spot serves delicious *petiscos* (tapas) – fava, ham and Serra cheese toast, pickled quail with fried bread, pork stew with pepper compote – followed by sweet endings like chestnut cake or quince crumble. The walls are clad with mismatching *azulejos* (hand-painted tiles), dining is at long communal tables, and there's a spirited rock 'n' roll vibe to the place. (📞213 971 504; www.petiscariaideal.com; Rua da Esperança 100; small plates €3-9, mains €9-14; ⏰7pm-2am Mon-Sat; 🛜)

Clube das Jornalistas

MEDITERRANEAN €€

12 🍴 MAP P134, F3

You have to be determined to find hilltop Clube das Jornalistas, but persevere. This 18th-century house, opening onto a tree-shaded courtyard, has oodles of charm and serves Mediterranean and Portuguese dishes such as creamy Brazilian-style shrimp-stew risotto and truffled black pork. The service is faultless, the food a worthy runner-up. (📞213 977 138; www.restauranteclubedejornalistas.com; Rua das Trinas 129; mains €15.50-23; ⏰12.30-2.30pm & 7.30pm-midnight Mon-Sat; 🛜)

Cantina Lx

CAFE €€

13 🍴 MAP P134, A5

Decked out like an industrial-chic country barn, this cool cafe in LX Factory is a laid-back pick for snacks, mains such as codfish and sirloin steak, and Sunday brunch. (www.cantinalx.com; Rua Rodrigues de Faria 103, LX Factory; mains €9-16.50; ⏰noon-3pm Mon, noon-3pm & 7.30pm-midnight Tue-Sat, to 4pm Sun; 🛜)

Loco

PORTUGUESE €€€

14 🍴 MAP P134, F2

In the shadow of the Basílica da Estrela, Lisbon's latest hot table comes courtesy of chef Alexandre Silva, whose bold and modern take on Portuguese cuisine taps both tradition and travel on its way to a personality-rich gastronomic adventure. It offers two daily-changing, description-free tasting menus (you choose 14 or 18 'moments'), each steeped in sustainability and seasonality. (📞213 951 861; www.loco.pt; Rua dos Navigantes 53B; dégustation from €90; ⏰7-11pm Tue-Sat)

1300 Taberna

PORTUGUESE €€€

15 🍴 MAP P134, A5

A hodgepodge mess of rustic-chic chandeliers and exposed air ducts hovers over large communal-table seating at this LX Factory favourite. It dishes out creative and fun takes on Portuguese fare, many from its wood-fired grill, and is one of the best places in LX

Factory for a drink. (☎213 649 170; www.1300taberna.com; Rua Rodrigues de Faria 103, LX Factory; mains €17-28; ⏰12.30-3pm & 8pm-midnight Tue-Sat; 🛜)

Drinking

Foxtrot

BAR

16 🚇 MAP P134, H1

A cuckoo-clock doorbell announces new arrivals to this dark, decadent slither of art-nouveau glamour, in the bar business since 1978. Foxtrot keeps the mood mellow with jazzy beats and excruciatingly attentive mixology detailed on a tracing-paper menu (cocktails €7 to €15). It's a wonderfully moody spot for a drink. (www.barfoxtrot.com; Tv Santa Teresa 28; ⏰6pm-2am Mon-Thu, to 3am Fri & Sat, 8pm-2am Sun; 🛜)

Quimera Brewpub

BREWERY

17 🚇 MAP P134, C4

An American-Brazilian couple launched Lisbon's second brewpub in 2016 with 12 brews, including rarer choices such as Belgian blonde ale, American dark lager and experimental sours, along with a few taps devoted to invited *lisboêta* suds from Dois Corvos, 8ª Colina, Lince and more. Downing proper pints within the Palácio das Necessidades' stone-walled 18th-century carriage tunnel feels vaguely medieval. (www.quimerabrewpub.com; Rua Prior do Crato 6; ⏰5pm-midnight Wed-Fri, to 2am Fri & Sat; 🛜)

Le Chat

BAR

18 🚇 MAP P134, E4

Staring at the view of the docks and Ponte 25 de Abril (and construction cranes!) is the prime activity on the terrace of this glass-walled cafe-bar. It's a casual spot for coffee by day or cocktails (€7.50 to €15) and mellow beats by night. Skip the food. (www.lechatlisboa.com; Jardim 9 de Abril, Rua das Janelas Verdes; ⏰12.30pm-2am Mon-Sat, to midnight Sun; 🛜)

Bosq

CLUB

19 🚇 MAP P134, B5

This hypercool two-storey nightclub features a 120-sq-metre vertical garden above the upstairs bar and duelling environments that bounce between dance, R&B and hip hop. Lisbon's bold and beautiful flock here to dance under the guise of nightlife-ready animal portraits and 3D wallpaper. (☎210 938 029; www.facebook.com/bosqlx; Rua Rodrigues de Faria 103, LX Factory; ⏰11pm-6am Fri & Sat)

Entertainment

Senhor Vinho

LIVE MUSIC

20 ⭐ MAP P134, F3

Fado star Maria da Fé owns this small place, welcoming first-rate *fadistas* (fado singers). Go for the fado (from 7pm) not the food, and feel free to refuse menu extras. (☎213 972 681; www.srvinho.com; Rua do Meio á Lapa 18; minimum €25; ⏰8pm-2am Mon-Sat)

Shopping

LX Market
MARKET

21 🏠 MAP P134, A5

Vintage clothing, antiques, crafts, food, and weird and wonderful plants – the LX Factory market is the place to find them.

Live music keeps the Sunday shoppers entertained. (www.lxmarket.com.pt; Rua Rodrigues de Faria 103, LX Factory; ⏰11am-8pm Sun)

Verso Branco
DESIGN

22 🏠 MAP P134, H3

'Free verse' is the name of this split-level design store, where Fernando has a story for every object.

The high-ceilinged space showcases Portuguese contemporary arts, crafts and furnishings, from Burel's quality wool creations to limited-edition La.Ga bags by designer Jorge Moita.

The beautifully crafted bags made from Tyvek weigh just 40g and can hold 55kg. (www.versobranco.pt; Rua da Boavista 132-134; ⏰11.30am-8pm Tue-Sat)

LX Factory

Tune into Lisbon's creative pulse at **LX Factory** (Map p134, A5; www.lxfactory.com; Rua Rodrigues de Faria 103), housed in a cavernous 19th-century industrial complex. Abandoned warehouses have been transformed into spaces for art studios, galleries, workshops, and printing and design companies. There's a rustically cool cafe as well as a bookshop, several restaurants, design-minded shops and cultural spaces. Throughout the month, you'll find a dynamic menu of events, from live concerts and film screenings to fashion shows and art exhibitions. Weekend nights see parties with a dance- and art-loving crowd.

Portugal Gifts
GIFTS & SOUVENIRS

23 🏠 MAP P134, E4

This craft shop puts a contemporary spin on Portuguese souvenirs, with everything from Barcelos cockerel mugs to *azulejo* coasters and chocolate sardines. (www.portugalgifts.com.pt; Rua Presidente Arriaga 60; ⏰10am-7pm Mon-Fri)

Worth a Trip 🔭
Palácio Nacional de Sintra

The icing on Sintra's Unesco World Heritage cake, this sugar-white palace, crowned by a pair of conical chimneys, is pure fantasy stuff. Of Moorish origins, the palace was expanded by Dom Dinis (1261–1325), then enlarged by João I in the 15th century and given a Manueline makeover in the following century. Take in arabesque courtyards, barley-twist columns and 15th- and 16th-century geometric tiles as you wander.

www.parquesdesintra.pt

adult/child €10/8.50

⏰9.30am-7pm

🚊 Trains to Sintra run half-hourly (hourly on weekends) from Rossio (€2.20, 40 minutes), and every 20 minutes from Oriente (half-hourly on weekends).

Capela Palatina

This simple Moorish chapel, founded by Dom Dinis in the early 14th century, holds visitors captive with its mosaic of polychrome, geometric tiles, flock of frescoed doves and – above all – intricately carved, kaleidoscopic wood ceiling.

Sala dos Cisnes

Over the years, Portuguese royals have thrown banquets, court dances and festivals in this grand hall. Its Renaissance-style gilded ceiling is adorned with frescos of 27 gold-collared *cisnes* (swans).

Sala das Pegas

Suspicious? You will be looking up at the ceiling frieze of *pegas* (magpies). Lore has it that the queen caught João I kissing one of her ladies-in-waiting. The king professed innocence and commissioned one magpie for every lady-in-waiting to stop their tittle-tattle. Each holds a ribbon in its beak with the words *por bem* ('for the good').

Palace Kitchen

Your gaze will be drawn to the palace's iconic 33m-high chimneys in the kitchen. Built in the 15th century by João I, a king with an appetite for hunting, it was perfect for cooking the game to be served at royal banquets.

Sala dos Brasões

No surface is left unadorned in this chamber. Blue-and-white 18th-century *azulejos* depicting vivid hunting scenes guide the eye to an octagonal dome ceiling, which is emblazoned with the shields of 72 leading 16th-century families.

★ Top Tips

o Arrive early or late to avoid the biggest crowds.

o Save on admission by buying a Parques da Sintra Monte da Lua combo ticket, which saves 5% to 10% depending on how many sites you choose.

o Guided tours (€5) run daily at 2.30pm.

✕ Take a Break

Since 1756, **Fábrica das Verdeiras Queijadas da Sapa** (www.facebook.com/queijadasdasapa; Alameda Volta do Duche 12; pastries from €0.85) has been rotting royal teeth with *queijadas*, pastry shells filled with a marzipan-like mix of fresh cheese, sugar, flour and cinnamon.

Casa Piriquita (www.piriquita.pt; Rua das Padarias 1-5; travesseiros €1.40) has been tempting locals with another luscious sweet since 1952: the *travesseiro*, a puff pastry filled with almond-and-egg-yolk cream.

Survival Guide

Before You Go 146

Book Your Stay 146

When to Go 146

Arriving in Lisbon 147

Aeroporto de Lisboa 147

Estação Santa Apolónia 147

Gare do Oriente 148

Getting Around 148

Metro 148

Tram, Bus & Funicular 148

Bicycle 148

Taxi & Ride-Share 149

Essential Information 149

Accessible Travel 149

Business Hours 149

Discount Cards 149

Electricity 150

Emergencies 150

Money 150

Public Holidays 150

Responsible Travel 150

Safe Travel 151

Toilets 151

Tourist Information 151

Ascensor da Bica (p41) MATT MUNRO/LONELY PLANET ©

Before You Go

Book Your Stay

○ Book ahead during high season (mid-July to mid-September).

○ Many guesthouses lack lifts, meaning you'll have to haul your luggage up three flights or more. If this disconcerts, be sure to book a place with a lift.

○ *Pensões* and *residenciais* are small-scale guesthouses, often with a personal feel. The best are generally better than the cheapest hotels. Rates usually include breakfast.

Useful Websites

Lisbon Lux (www. lisbonlux.com) Hip local guide to all things Lisbon, including accommodation of all types.

Go Lisbon (www. golisbon.com) Local guide with hotels, apartments, hostels and *pousadas* (upmarket inns) divided by various categories of interest.

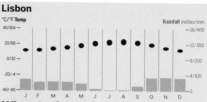

Lisbon

°C/°F Temp / Rainfall inches/mm

When to Go

Winter (Nov–Feb) Quiet except for Carnival in February. Low-season deals available. Weather can be wet and windy.

Spring (Mar–May) Parks in bloom, mild and often sunny days, accommodation still reasonably priced – perfect season for exploring.

Summer (Jun–Aug) Usually hot. Best time for open-air festivals, beach days and alfresco dining. Rooms are at a premium; book ahead.

Autumn (Sep–Oct) Pleasant temps, culture-focused events and few crowds, though showers are to be expected.

Lonely Planet (www. lonelyplanet.com/ portugal/lisbon/hotels) Recommendations and bookings.

Best Budget

Lisbon Calling (www. lisboncalling.net) A lovely Santa Catarina backpackers with original frescos, *azulejos* and hardwood floors.

Lisbon Destination Hostel (www. destinationhostels. com) World-class hostel housed in Lisbon's loveliest train station.

Home Lisbon Hostel (www.homelisbon hostel.com) Family-run hostel in the heart of Baixa with top-end facilities.

Independente (www. theindependente.pt) Stylish boutique option across from the dramatic Miradouro de São Pedro de Alcântara.

Living Lounge (www. livingloungehostel.com) Straddling Chiado and Baixa, and steeped in vintage cool, this social hostel oozes restrained hipness.

Best Midrange

Casa do Príncipe
(www.casadoprincipe.
com) Excellent-value
nine-room B&B oc-
cupying a 19th-century
neo-Moorish palace.

**Lisbon Story Guest-
house** (www.lisbon
storyguesthouse.com)
Wonderful guesthouse
with themed rooms
overlooking lively Largo
de São Domingos.

Casa Amora (www.
casaamora.com)
Discerning and stylish
boutique hotel with
lovely gardens and per-
sonalised service near
historic Mãe d'Água.

Lisbon Dreams (www.
lisbondreamsguest
house.com) Tasteful
high-ceilinged rooms.

Casa de São Mamede
(www.casadesao
mamede.com) Near the
botanical gardens, this
18th-century, family
run villa has rooms set
with period furnishings.

Best Top End

Palácio Belmonte
(www.palaciobelmonte.
com) Idyllic 15th-cen-
tury luxury palace near
Castelo de São Jorge.

Santiago de Alfama
(www.santiagode
alfama.com) A ruined
15th-century palace
turned boutique gem in
Alfama.

Valverde (www.
valverdehotel.com)
Exquisitely curated,
high-design 25-room
boutique inside a
luxury converted town
house on Avenida da
Liberdade.

Memmo Alfama (www.
memmoalfama.com)
Trendy boutique hotel
with stunning views
over Alfama from its
roof terrace.

Pestana Palace Lisboa
(www.pestana.com/
pt/hotel/pestana
-palace) Italian archi-
tect Nicola Bigaglia's
1904 Valle Flor Palace –
a National Monument –
houses this historically
stunning hotel.

Arriving in Lisbon

Aeroporto de Lisboa

○ Around 6km north of
the centre, the ultra-
modern Aeroporto de
Lisboa operates direct
flights to major interna-
tional hubs.

○ The airport is con-
nected to central Lisbon
by metro (a single costs
€1.45). It is the terminus
of the red line.

○ The **AeroBus** (www.
yellowbustours.com;
one-way €3.60) departs
from outside the arriv-
als hall roughly every
20 minutes from 7am
to 11pm. It goes via
Marquês de Pombal,
Avenida da Liberdade,
Restauradores, Rossio
and Praça do Comércio
to Cais do Sodré (25 to
35 minutes). The ticket
gives free passage on
the city bus network for
the rest of the day.

○ A taxi into central Lisbon should cost around
€16, plus €1.60 for lug-
gage. Avoid queues by
flagging one down at the
departures hall.

Estação Santa Apolónia

○ Metro services run
every few minutes, pro-
viding speedy connec-
tions to central Lisbon. A
single ticket costs €1.45
to anywhere in the city.

○ Santa Apolónia is on
the blue line, one stop
from Terreiro do Paço
(Praça do Comércio),
the heart of downtown
Lisbon.

Gare do Oriente

○ The ultramodern Gare do Oriente is on the red metro line, which provides quick and frequent connections to central Lisbon.

○ Baixa-Chiado in central Lisbon is a 20-minute metro ride away. Change for the green line at Alameda.

○ Bus services linking Gare do Oriente to central Lisbon include the 708 to Martim Moniz (via the airport). Single tickets cost €1.85.

Getting Around

Metro

○ Compact and easy to navigate, the Lisbon Metro (www.metro lisboa.pt) has just four lines: red, green, yellow and blue.

○ The metro runs from 6.30am to 1am.

○ Buy tickets from the machines at metro stations; a single costs €1.45.

○ Validate your ticket at the station entrance.

○ Useful signs include '*correspondência*' (transfer between lines) and '*saída*' (exit to the street).

Tram, Bus & Funicular

○ Carris (www.carris.pt) operates all transport except the metro.

○ Buses and trams run from about 5am or 6am to 1am; there are some night bus and tram services.

○ Pick up a transport map from tourist offices or Carris kiosks, which are dotted around the city. The Carris website has timetables and route details.

○ Individual tickets cost €1.85 on buses, €2.90 on trams; they can be purchased on board. Buy 24-hour Carris passes (€6.15) from ticket machines or kiosks at metro stations.

○ A return funicular journey costs €3.70, except the Elevador de Santa Justa, which costs €5.15.

○ Always validate your ticket.

Bicycle

○ Traffic, trams, hills and cobbles make cycling a challenging prospect. There are pleasant rides along a bike lane beside the Rio Tejo, however.

Tickets & Passes

There are two useful cards for catching public transport around the city; both can be purchased from kiosks in the metro stations.

Viva Viagem/7 Colinas Costs €0.50, to which you can then add credit in various denominations. Select the 'add credit' option, rather than a single trip (only valid for the metro), which allows the card to be used on the metro, buses, trams and funiculars. Pay-as-you go fares are €1.30 on metro and Carris (buses and trams).

24-hour Carris/metro pass Costs €6.30 and allows unlimited travel over a 24-hour period on all buses, trams, funiculars and the metro.

o A handy place to rent bikes is **Bike Iberia** ([phone] 969 630 369; www. bikeiberia.com; Largo Corpo Santo 5; bike hire per hour/day from €5/15, e-bike per hour/day €20/35; [clock]9.30am-7pm), a short stroll from Cais do Sodré.

o For shorter trips, you can use **Gira** ([phone]211 163 060; www.gira-bicicletas delisboa.pt; per 45min €2; [clock]6am-2am), the city's bike-sharing scheme, with at least 50 stations around the city.

Taxi & Ride-Share

o Taxis in Lisbon are plentiful. Try the ranks at Rossio and Praça dos Restauradores, near stations and ferry terminals.

o The starting fare on the meter should read €3.25 (daytime flag fall).

o You will be charged extra for luggage and 20% more for journeys from 9pm to 6am.

o Many locals prefer to use taxi apps and ride-share services, which are markedly cheaper than conventional taxis.

o A few popular apps include Uber (www. uber.com), Cabify

(www.cabify.com), 99Taxis (www.99taxis. com), Taxify (www. taxify.eu) and MyTaxi (https://pt.mytaxi.com).

Essential Information

Accessible Travel

Lisbon's airport is wheelchair accessible. Newer hotels tend to have some adapted rooms, though the facilities may not be up to scratch; some hostels have facilities for people with disabilities.

Lisbon, with its cobbled streets and hills, may be difficult for travellers with disabilities, but not impossible. Baixa's flat grid and Belém are fine, and all the sights at Parque das Nações are accessible.

Download Lonely Planet's free Accessible Travel guides from http://lptravel.to/AccessibleTravel.

Accessible Portugal ([phone] 211 338 693; www.acc essibleportugal.com; Rua António Champalimaud,

Lote 1) This Lisbon-based association promotes accessible tourism and is the brains behind the excellent **TUR4all Portugal** app (Android and iOS), which works like a database of accessible tourist resources and services throughout Portugal and Spain.

Business Hours

Many shops close on Sundays and some shut early on Saturdays; small boutiques may also close for lunch (1pm to 3pm). Many museums are closed on Mondays.

Restaurants noon to 3pm and 7pm to 10pm

Cafes 8am to midnight

Shops 9.30am to 7pm Monday to Friday, to 1pm Saturday

Bars 7pm to 3am

Nightclubs 11pm to 6am Thursday to Saturday

Banks 8.30am to 3pm Monday to Friday

Discount Cards

The **Lisboa Card** offers unlimited use of public transport (including trains to Sintra and Cascais), entry to all key museums and attractions, and discounts of up to 50% on tours, cruises and other admission charges. It's available at **Ask Me Lisboa tourist offices** (☎210 312 810; www.askmelisboa. com; Praça do Comércio; ☻9am-8pm), including the one at the **airport** (☎218 450 660; www. askmelisboa.com; Aeroporto de Lisboa, Arrivals Hall; ☻7am-midnight). The 24-/48-/72-hour versions cost €19/32/40. You validate the card when you want to start using it.

Electricity

Type C
230V/50Hz

Type F
230V/50Hz

Emergencies

Police, fire and ambulance (☎112)

Money

Currency

The Portuguese currency is the euro (€), divided into 100 cents.

ATMS

ATMs (Multibancos) are the easiest way to access your money. You just need your card and PIN.

Your home bank will usually charge around 1.5% per transaction.

Credit Cards

Visa is widely accepted, as is MasterCard. American Express and Diners Club less so, with the exception of at top-end hotels and restaurants.

Tipping

Service is not usually added to the bill. In touristy areas,10% is fine, though it's never expected (few Portuguese ever leave more than a round-up to the nearest euro).

Public Holidays

Banks, offices, department stores and some shops close on public holidays.

Responsible Travel

○ Travel off-season: outside the busiest periods (May to September and Easter), and midweek instead of weekends.

○ Travel green. Skip the bus tours and opt for walking and biking excursions instead.

○ Consider including a side trip to parts of Portugal not suffering from overtourism, such as Beja, Serpa, Castro

Money-Saving Tips

o If you're on a budget, save your sightseeing for Sunday mornings, when entry to the majority of Lisbon's museums is free.

o Most sights have concessions (up to 50%) for youths, students and seniors – make sure you bring appropriate ID.

o Lisbon's top sights and attractions usually offer free entry for children under 12 (occasionally under 14).

Verde and other places in the Alentejo.

o Lend a hand. At **Refood Nossa Senhora de Fátima** (www.facebook .com/refoodnsradefatima), you can help serve food to those in need.

Safe Travel

Lisbon generally enjoys a low crime rate, but petty theft is on the rise.

o Mind your wallet on trams – major hotspots for pickpockets – and other tourist hubs such as Rua Augusta.

o Pay attention at night around Anjos, Martim Moniz and Intendente metro stations, where muggings have occurred. Take care in dark alleys around Alfama and Graça.

o Always keep your wits about you in Cais do Sodré, which has seen an increase in snatch-and-grabs.

Toilets

Public toilets in Lisbon are rare. Train, metro and bus stations generally have public conveniences. Your best bet is to pop into the nearest cafe or bar. If you just want to use the loo, order a *bica* (espresso) – one of the cheapest things on the menu.

Tourist Information
Central Offices

Palácio Foz (213 463 314; www.askmelisboa.com; Praça dos Restauradores; 9am-8pm) Lisbon's

largest and most helpful tourist office. Has maps and information, and books accommodation and rental cars. Also provides left luggage and charged internet access.

Terreiro do Paço (210 312 810; Praça do Comércio; 9am-8pm) Another helpful branch. These are all run by the city's official tourism arm, Turismo de Lisboa, but bear in mind it is member-driven so not impartial when it comes to recommendations.

Information Kiosks

Aeroporto de Lisboa (218 450 660; Arrivals Hall; 7am-midnight)

Belém (910 517 981; Mosteiro dos Jerónimos; 9am-6pm)

Torre de Belém (910 517 886; Jardim da Torre de Belém; 9am-6pm)

Rossio (910 517 914; Praça Dom Pedro IV; 10am-1pm & 2-6pm)

Language

Most sounds in Portuguese are also found in English. The exceptions are the nasal vowels (represented in our pronunciation guides by '*ng*' after the vowel), pronounced as if you're trying to make the sound through your nose; and the strongly rolled *r* (represented by '*rr*' in our pronunciation guides). The symbol '*zh*' sounds like the 's' in 'pleasure'. Keeping these points in mind and reading the pronunciation guides as if they were English, you'll be understood just fine. The stressed syllables are indicated with italics. To enhance your trip with a phrasebook, visit lonelyplanet.com. Lonely Planet iPhone phrasebooks are available through the Apple App store.

Basics

Hello.
Olá.　　　　　o·*laa*

Goodbye.
Adeus.　　　　a·de·*oosh*

How are you?
Como está?　　ko·moo *shtaa*

Fine, and you?
Bem, e você?　　beng e vo·*se*

Please.
Por favor.　　　poor fa·*vor*

Thank you.
Obrigado. (m)　o·bree·*gaa*·doo
Obrigada. (f)　o·bree·*gaa*·da

Excuse me.
Faz favor.　　　faash fa·*vor*

Sorry.
Desculpe.　　　desh·*kool*·pe

Yes./No.
Sim./Não.　　　seeng/nowng

I don't understand.
Não entendo.　　nowng eng·*teng*·doo

Do you speak English?
Fala inglês?　　faa·la eeng·*glesh*

Eating & Drinking

..., please. *..., por favor.* ..., poor fa·*vor*

A coffee　*Um café*　　oong ka·*fe*

A table　*Uma mesa*　oo·ma me·za
for two　*para duas*　pa·ra oo·ash
　　　　　pessoas　　pe·so·ash

Two
beers　　*Dois*　　　doysh
　　　　　cervejas　　ser·*ve*·zhash

I'm a vegetarian.
Eu sou　　　　　e·oo soh
vegetariano/　　ve·zhe·a·ree·a·noo/
vegetariana. (m/f) ve·zhe·a·ree·a·na

Cheers!
Saúde!　　　　　sa·oo·de

That was delicious!
Isto estava　　　eesh·too shtaa·va
delicioso.　　　de·lee·see·o·zoo

The bill, please.
A conta, por favor.　a *kong*·ta poor
　　　　　　　　fa·*vor*

Shopping

I'd like to buy ...
Queria　　　　　ke·*ree*·a
comprar ...　　　kong·*praar* ...

I'm just looking.
Estou só a ver.　shtoh so a ver

How much is it?

Quanto custa?	kwang·too koosh·ta

It's too expensive.

Está muito caro.	shtaa mweeng·too kaa·roo

Can you lower the price?

Pode baixar o preço?	po·de bai·shaar oo pre·soo

Emergencies

Help!

Socorro!	soo·ko·rroo

Call a doctor!

Chame um médico!	shaa·me oong me·dee·koo

Call the police!

Chame a polícia!	shaa·me a poo·lee·sya

I'm sick.

Estou doente.	shtoh doo·eng·te

I'm lost.

Estou perdido. (m)	shtoh per·dee·doo
Estou perdida. (f)	shtoh per·dee·da

Where's the toilet?

Onde é a casa de de banho?	ong·de e a kaa·za ba·nyoo

Time & Numbers

What time is it?

Que horas são?	kee o·rash sowng

It's (10) o'clock.

São (dez) horas.	sowng (desh) o·rash

Half past (10).

(Dez) e meia.	(desh) e may·a

morning	*manhã*	ma·nyang
afternoon	*tarde*	taar·de
evening	*noite*	noy·te
yesterday	*ontem*	ong·teng
today	*hoje*	o·zhe
tomorrow	*amanhã*	aa·ma·nyang
1	*um*	oong
2	*dois*	doysh
3	*três*	tresh
4	*quatro*	kwaa·troo
5	*cinco*	seeng·koo
6	*seis*	saysh
7	*sete*	se·te
8	*oito*	oy·too
9	*nove*	no·ve
10	*dez*	desh

Transport & Directions

Where's ...?

Onde é ...?	ong·de e ...

What's the address?

Qual é o endereço?	kwaal e oo eng·de·re·soo

Can you show me (on the map)?

Pode-me mostrar (no mapa)?	po·de·me moosh·traar (noo maa·pa)

When's the next bus?

Quando é que sai o próximo autocarro?	kwang·doo e ke sai oo pro·see·moo ow·to·kaa·rroo

I want to go to ...

Queria ir a ...	ke·ree·a eer a ...

Does it stop at ...?

Pára em ...?	paa·ra eng ...

Please stop here.

Por favor pare aqui.	poor fa·vor paa·re a·kee

Behind the Scenes

Send Us Your Feedback

We love to hear from travellers – your comments help make our books better. We read every word, and we guarantee that your feedback goes straight to the authors. Visit **lonelyplanet.com/contact** to submit your updates and suggestions.

Note: We may edit, reproduce and incorporate your comments in Lonely Planet products such as guidebooks, websites and digital products, so let us know if you don't want your comments reproduced or your name acknowledged. For a copy of our privacy policy visit lonelyplanet.com/privacy.

Acknowledgements

Cover photographs: (front) View of Lisbon with the Castelo de São Jorge, SeanPavonePhoto/ Getty Images ©; (back) Floor tiles, Rossio, Lisbon, Travel Faery/ Shutterstock ©

Photographs pp28–9 (from left): Gustavo Frazao; trabantos; Sean Pavone; StockPhotosArt; Radu Bercan/Shutterstock ©

This Book

This 5th edition of Lonely Planet's *Pocket Lisbon* guidebook was curated by Regis St Louis and researched and written by Kevin Raub, who also researched the 4th edition. The first three editions were researched and written by Kerry Christiani. This guidebook was produced by the following:

Destination Editor
Tom Stainer

Senior Product Editors
Daniel Bolger, Genna Patterson

Product Editors
Kirsten Rawlings, Hannah Cartmel

Senior Cartographers
Hunor Csutoros, Anthony Phelan

Book Designers Katherine Marsh, Lauren Egan

Assisting Editors
Will Allen, Janet Austin, Nigel Chin

Assisting Cartographer
Rachel Imeson

Cover Researcher
Fergal Condon

Thanks to Sandra Henriques Gajjar, Anne Mason, Kate Mathews, Rachel Rawling

Index

⊗ Eating

Our

Regis has contributed to more than 50 Lonely Plan
titles, covering destinations across six continents.
His travels have taken him from the mountains of
Kamchatka to remote island villages in Melanesia,
and to many grand urban landscapes. Follow him o
Instagram @regisstlouis.

Kevin Raub

Atlanta native Kevin started his career as a music
journalist in New York, working for *Men's Journal* an
Rolling Stone magazines. He ditched the rock 'n' ro
lifestyle for travel writing and has written nearly 50
Lonely Planet guides, focused mainly on Brazil, Ch
Colombia, USA, India, the Caribbean and Portugal.
Along the way, the self-confessed hophead is in co
stant search of wildly high IBUs in local beers. Follo
him on Twitter and Instagram @raubontheroad.

Published by Lonely Planet Global Limited

CRN 554153
5th edition – Feb 2022
ISBN 978 1 78868 044 8
© Lonely Planet 2022 Photographs © as indicated 2022
10 9 8 7 6 5 4 3 2 1
Printed in Singapore